What is Truth?

Dedicated to Peter Rodwell,
A good friend,
And a true Christian.

Books available from:

USA   Alan Ames Ministry
             PO Box 200
             233 Glasgow Avenue SW
             Kellogg
             Minnesota 55945
Phone: 507 767 3027

AUSTRALIA   Touch of Heaven
             (Alan Ames Ministry)
             PO Box 85
             Wembley, 6014
             West Australia
Phone: 61 89275 6608
Fax: 61 89382 4392
Web: http://www.alanames.ws
Email: alan@alanames.ws

The decree of the Congregation of the Propagation of the Faith, A.A.S 58, 1186 (approved by Pope Paul VI on October 14, 1966) states that the Nihil Obstat and Imprimatur are no longer required on publications that deal with private revelations, provided that they contain nothing contrary to faith and morals.

The publisher recognizes and accepts that the final authority regarding the events described in this book rests with the Holy See of Rome, to whose judgement we willingly submit.

All Holy Scripture references are taken from The New American Bible.

Sections of this book may not be copied without permission of the author.

Copyright Carver Alan Ames-2004

CONTENTS

	page
Preface	6
Introduction	9
The Church	10
Structure of the Church	12
Authority of the Church	14
Authority of Peter	15
Churches and People	18
Church and State	21
Church Scandals	23
Riches of the Church	26
The Sacraments	28
Baptism	29
Confirmation	32
The Eucharist	34
Reconciliation	39
Predestination	45
Anointing of the Sick	46
Holy Orders	48
Are all Priests?	49
Homosexuality and the Priesthood	51
Women Priests and Women's Role in the Church	52
Married Priests	54
Marriage	57
Homosexuality	63
Contraception	66
IVF	71
Mary	73
Repetitious Prayer	78
Statues	79
Venerating Saints	80
Praying to Saints	81
Purgatory	83
Speaking to the Dead	85
Faith	87
Tradition	90
Other Faiths	93
Tolerance Between Faiths	95
War	97
Sanctity of Life	101
End Times	103
Antichrist	106
Signs and Wonders	107
Mini-Judgement	108
Summary	109

PREFACE

(Jn 18:37-38 Jesus answered, 'You say I am a king. For this I was born and for this I came into the world, to testify to the truth. Every one who belongs to the truth listens to my voice.' Pilate said to him, 'What is truth?')

The question that Pontius Pilate asked the Lord has been repeated many times in the history of the Church. From the Church's beginnings, through history to the Church's councils where our faith was defined as dogma, to the Reformation where the great protest began, through to this modern age where ancient but false philosophies have gained popularity, people have remained the same. As we search for meaning to our existence we ask the age-old question: where does the *truth* lie?

That is where our Christian faith comes to the fore, because it is by faith that we can answer this very complex question. Faith is not something we can learn from an intellectual reading of the Scriptures or attending a Catholic school or attending Sunday school every week or even achieving a Bachelor's degree in Theology. No, faith is a gift from God, a gift freely offered to all but a gift that has to be nurtured through an open and receptive heart.

If we are to be *on the side of truth*, then we have to *listen to the Lord's voice*. The Church has endured for two thousand years as the Lord promised it would: *(Mt 16: 18 The gates of the netherworld shall not prevail against it)*. The Lord has given us the Sacraments and we have the Communion of Saints, that great company of witnesses who have left us a treasure of spiritual experience and a significant bank of examples of how to trust in the Lord.

The Church that Christ himself established to be the enduring rock of truth - the truth of what God is calling us to - remains to guide us as we ask the Lord to strengthen our faith in the eternal life that he offers us all. Thanks be to God for His great mercy and love.

- Fr Richard Rutkauskas -

Books and Tapes available by C.A.Ames

Title	Price US $
Through the Eyes of Jesus, Trilogy	26.00
Through the Eyes of Jesus, Vol 1	8.00
Through the Eyes of Jesus, Vol 2	8.00
Through the Eyes of Jesus, Vol 3	8.00
Heaven Speaks	10.00
Messages to Carver Alan Ames	10.00
Our Father Speaks	12.00
Stories of Love	11.00
The Way of Hope	8.00
Salaam Shalom	10.00
Our Mother's Heart	10.00

Vidoes, Audios & Rosary available by C.A.Ames

Through His Eyes, Focus Video 1	20.00
Revelations from Heaven, Focus Video 2	20.00
Touching Lives, Touching Souls, Focus Video	20.00
Three Focus Videos	50.00
Come Back to God, Video	20.00
Why God? Vol 1, Video	15.00
Why God? Vol 2, Video	15.00
Why God? Both videos	25.00
Audio Tape	3.00
Eucharistic Rosary Package (Inc. Rosary Beads)	2.00

Introduction

Many people wonder about the true faith Our Lord Jesus Christ gave to mankind. They wonder what is true and what it is they should follow and accept as truth. What it is they should live to.

Among the various Christian denominations and people, questions arise about the differences some churches have. In this book, by the grace of God, some of these differences will be faced honestly and answered in truth so as to help each person who reads it see more clearly what Our Lord truly gave to us and asks of us in this life.

The answers will come from the teachings Our Lord has given to me and from Holy Scripture. There is no intention of condemning or belittling anyone's beliefs, only the desire that all may come to know more intimately the full truth of Our Lord and His divine desire for each person.

I pray that all my brothers and sisters in Christ Our Lord, no matter what path they may be walking, will read this book with an open heart, mind and soul. Then, that through this openness, the Holy Spirit will be invited within so as to bring the knowledge of what is truth into each one.

The Church

The starting point naturally should be to look at the Church God gave to mankind in His Son and Our Lord Jesus. The Church, which is the body of Christ.

Some say the Church began at Pentecost when the Holy Spirit descended upon the apostles. However, as the Church is the body of Christ then surely the Church began when Christ Our Lord came to earth.

In that divine moment mankind was permitted by God's grace to see the fullness of His love and in that divine moment the human being was given the way to live, the way to follow and the way to Heaven.

It was also in that sacred time through Mary the mother of Jesus and in her suffering, people were shown they too would be called to suffer if they wanted to have Christ alive within them. In Mary was a sign of the suffering and sacrificial Church our Lord was giving to mankind in Himself. Mary, with total obedience to God's will, accepted whatever He asked of her and endured whatever was necessary so that God's will could be done in her life.

This was a sign for all to follow if they truly wanted God to reign supreme in their lives. In following this sign, just as the Son of God was alive in Mary during her pregnancy, united in her being, people can find Our Lord Jesus alive in them and find themselves united in Him. Through the suffering people endure or the sacrifices some have to make for the love of God, God will build up His Church and will reach out to touch sinners and convert them. In this, people are also called to have obedience to the will of God otherwise what is built up is not of God but of man.

Later, when Our Lord began His public ministry the Holy Spirit was seen to descend upon Him. Here Our Lord, who is the head of the Church *(Col 1:18 He is the head of the body, the church)* and whose body is the

Church, was showing all that is done in Him, through Him, and with Him, is done in, through, and with the Holy Spirit, who is one with Him. Here Christ Our Lord, who is the Church which we are called to be part of, part of His body, *(1 Corin 12:27 You are Christ's body and individually parts of it)* is reminding people that the Church is filled with and guided by the Holy Spirit *(Jn 16:13 The spirit of truth he will guide you to all truth)*. Everything people do within the Church should be done in the Spirit of God and not in the spirit of the world. As part of Christ's body, all should be desiring by the power of His Holy Spirit to be like Him in all things and to be obedient to Him in all things. That, just as the Lord Jesus is one with the Father and Holy Spirit, all in the Church are called to be one in Him. So that through Him all can experience oneness with God and find the intimate and personal relationship God wants all to have with Him. Our Lord prayed for this *(Jn 17:20-21 I pray-so that they all may be one, as you, Father, are in me and I in you, that they also may be in us)*.

However, today the Christian churches are many and often the churches fight amongst themselves, accuse and condemn each other, reject each other and do not see that in doing so they are no longer one in Christ Our Lord but many in the worldly ways and pride-filled ways of mankind.

The Church Our Lord gave to His people was by His divine will to be one in Him *(Jn 10:16 There will be one flock, one shepherd)* confirmed by God's Word through St Paul *(Eph 4:4-5 One body, one spirit called to one hope - one Lord, one faith, one baptism)*.

Structure of Church

How, then, has it come to be that more than one church exists in His name when this is not what Our Lord wanted?

It is important to look at how the Lord built the Church and how He asks us to live obediently within His Church which has His authority.

Our Lord, in His divine wisdom and love, a wisdom and love that is far greater than any other, a wisdom and love where all other true wisdom and love comes from, chose His apostles upon which to build His Church *(Eph 2:20 Built on the foundation of the apostles and prophets. Jn 15:16 It was not you who chose me but I who chose you and appointed you to go and bear fruit that will remain).*

So it must follow that His Church must be an apostolic one given by Christ through His apostles for all people. Our Lord appointed the apostles to carry on His mission of love *(Jn 20:21 As the Father has sent me, so I send you)* to build His body of love, His Church for all people so all can become one in His love, one in His Church, one in His kingdom.

From amongst the apostles, in His divine wisdom, Our Lord chose Peter to lead His Church. Peter was the God-given rock upon which the Church would be built *(Mt 16:18 So I say to you, you are Peter and upon this rock I will build my church).* Peter, chosen by God and accepted by the apostles as the Lord's appointed leader. Peter, appointed to strengthen his brothers' faith *(Luke 22:32 You must strengthen your brothers).* Our Lord Jesus said to all that there will be one shepherd to lead the flock and in His choosing of Peter as the rock upon which His Church is to be built and the leader to strengthen the faith, Our Lord said to all, here is My chosen shepherd *(Jn 21:17 (Jesus) said to him: "Feed my sheep").*

With these acts the Lord was putting in place the hierarchical structure of His Church. Peter as the leader, the apostles, brothers of Peter and leaders in their own right, but they themselves led, strengthened, and fed by Peter. St Paul in his letter to the Ephesians gave an insight into the hierarchical structure of the Church *(Eph 4:11 And he gave some as apostles, others as prophets, others as evangelists, others as pastors and teachers).* In his letter to Timothy, St Paul identifies the role of bishops, priests and deacons *(1 Tim 3:1 Whoever aspires to the office of bishop desires a noble task. 1 Tim 3:8 Similarly, deacons must be dignified.*

1 Tim 5:17 Presbyters who preside well deserve double honour, especially those who toil in preaching and teaching). While in the letter to Titus is the commission for bishops to ordain priests *(Titus 1:5 And appoint presbyters in every town).*

God gave mankind the Church in this way because God knows mankind's weaknesses and He knows that unless guided correctly, in the way God wants, that mankind's pride will lead it astray. So Our Lord set in place the structure of love, the structure of faith, the structure of hope which is to be His Holy Apostolic Church to lead mankind into His glorious and eternal kingdom of heaven *(Eph 2:21 Through him the whole structure is held together and grows into a temple sacred in the Lord).*

<u>Authority of the Church</u>

It follows as Our Lord placed St Peter in charge of His Church, then the authority of Christ was given to St Peter and also to the apostles who were there to help form the Church and help the Church grow. In His own words Our Lord gives this authority to the apostles *(Mt 18:18 Amen, I say to you, whatever you bind on earth shall be bound in heaven and whatever you loose on earth shall be loosed in heaven)*. With these divine words the Lord was saying to all who would listen that everyone must follow the teachings of the Apostolic Church, accept the God-given authority of the Church and be obedient to the Church.

Not doing so brings people to reject and deny the word of God in Holy Scripture and also the Word of God through His Holy Apostolic Church *(Luke 10:16 Whoever listens to you, listens to me. Whoever rejects you, rejects me and whoever rejects me rejects the one who sent me)*. The giving of authority to the Apostolic Church is also confirmed in the way the Lord sent the apostles out to the world *(Mt 28:18-20 All power in heaven and on earth has been given to me. Go therefore and make disciples of all nations, baptizing them in the name of the Father, and the Son, and the Holy Spirit. Teaching them to observe all I have commanded you. Jn 20:21 As the Father has sent me so I send you)*.

Authority of Peter

This God-given authority, especially in the case of St Peter whose name always heads the list of apostles in Holy Scripture, and his successors, is often questioned and sometimes denied. Some even call the Pope the Antichrist, yet ignore in Holy Scripture, in the Holy

Word of God, the authority that was given. In doing so, in rejecting the word, the authority of Christ Our Lord, then people stand against His Word, His authority and in some way are antichrist themselves.

The Lord spoke on St Peter's leadership *(Mt 16:18-19 I say to you, you are Peter and upon this rock I will build my church, and the gates of the netherworld shall not prevail against it. I will give you the keys to the kingdom of heaven. Whatever you bind on earth shall be bound in heaven; whatever you loose on earth shall be loosed in heaven. Jn 21:15-17 "Feed my lambs." "Tend my sheep." "Feed my sheep." Luke 22:32 You must strengthen your brothers)*.

In the Acts of the Apostles there are several instances where the leadership of St Peter was shown *(Acts 1:13-26 St Peter headed the meeting at which Matthias was elected. Acts 2:14 St Peter led the apostles in preaching at Pentecost. Acts 2:41 Received first converts who had accepted his message. Acts 3:6-7 St Peter performed the first miracle after Pentecost with the cure of the crippled beggar. Acts 15 St Peter led the first council and also made first dogmatic decision which was then supported by the apostles and the whole church)*.

St Paul, with his visit to St Peter after his conversion, *(Gal 1:18 I went up to Jerusalem to confer with Kephas and remained with him for fifteen days)* showed once more the leadership position of St Peter. Some say that because St Paul *(Gal 2:11 And when Kephas came to Antioch I opposed him to his face because he clearly was wrong)* opposed St Peter to his face this was a rejection of St Peter's primacy. Yet, nowhere did St Paul deny St Peter as leader. Yes, he pointed out where he thought St Peter had made a mistake, but he did not question St Peter's authority. This is a sign for all the Church that when there seems to be a mistake within the Church people can stand up and discuss this with the desire to correct any wrong that may occur. However, St Paul did not leave the Church or divide the Church. Instead, he continued working to build the Church and to build unity within it. Another sign that this is what all who love Our Lord Jesus are called to do *(Eph 4:3-5 Striving to preserve the unity of the spirit through the bond of peace - one body and one spirit, one Lord, one faith, one baptism. Col 3:15 Called in one body).*

Each member of the Church is called to unite, to strengthen and to help the Church grow. To do this it is essential that each one bows to the will of God, bows to the authority of God and not to the will of man. It will happen from time to time that misunderstandings occur within the Church and that yes, mistakes will occur too. However, what each person should keep in mind is that the Church is the body of Christ, it is filled with the Holy Spirit and that when misunderstandings or mistakes happen God in His time and in His way will correct them. What God asks from each person is of course to stand up for what is right but to do so, not in anger, not in frustration, not in a desire to hurt the Church. But to do so in confidence that God has everything in hand. To do so gently, lovingly, forgivingly and kindly. To pray for the wrongs to be righted. To pray that through the time of trial the Church may be going through the Church will come out of it stronger and holier.

Each person should try to see times like these as tests of faith and tests of obedience. In these times if a person trusts completely in God to correct any mistake and offers the difficulties, even the sufferings they may be going through because of this, to God in love, then God uses these sacrifices to pour out grace to strengthen the Church and the person. Not doing this can lead people into a weakness of faith that can take them into disobedience to God's chosen one and so to disobedience to God's will. It is in these times that Satan works his wiles trying to lead people into doubt, into uncertainty, into confusion and into disobedience. Satan sees these times as opportunities to divide and weaken God's Church. It is in these times people need to make a special effort to trust in God that His will be done.

Churches and People

Some accept the primacy of St Peter but do not accept his successors and the passing of leadership to them or accept the apostolic succession of the bishops.

However, even in the Old Testament God was explaining there is to be a high priest *(2 Chr 19:11 High priest over you in everything that pertains to the Lord)* and in the New Testament *(Heb 5:1-2 Every high priest is taken from among men and made their representative before God to offer gifts and sacrifices for sins. He is able to deal patiently with the ignorant and erring for he himself is beset by weakness. Heb 5:4 No one takes this honour upon himself but only when called by God, just as Aaron was).* That the priests are an essential and necessary part of the Church as messengers of the Lord, there to guide people on the right way *(Mal 2:7 For the lips of the priests are to keep knowledge, and instruction is to be sought from his mouth, because he is the messenger of the Lord of hosts)* and the sacred gifts of the Holy Spirit are also given through the priests by their laying on of hands *(1 Tim 4:14 The gift you have which was conferred on you through the prophetic word with the imposition of hands of the presbyterate)* showing the priests are vessels and servants of the Holy Spirit through whom His divine grace is poured out so the Church can continue in its missionary role.

After the death, resurrection and ascension of Our Lord to Heaven, the apostolic succession of the Church was confirmed with the selection of Matthias to replace the Apostle Judas who had betrayed Our Lord *(Acts 1:20 May another take his office. Acts 1:25 To take the place in this apostolic ministry).* With this apostolic succession in place St Paul reminds all that God has chosen the apostles to be first in the Church *(1 Corin 12:28 Some people God has designated in the church to be, first, apostles).*

There is a belief the Church should be a democracy but if it is to remain God's Church, this cannot be. The Church is a Theocracy with God at the head *(Col 1:18 He is the head of the body, the church)* ruling with benevolent love, ruling with mercy and compassion, ruling with truth, but always ruling. When a church becomes a democracy, it becomes the church of man and not of God because now man's will rules the church and not God's will.

It is also suggested that temporal authorities, i.e. kings, princes, governments, are to play a role in governing the Church *(1 Peter 2:13-15 Be subjected to every human institution, for the Lord's sake whether it be to the king, as supreme, or to the governors - for it is the will of God).* Martin Luther (An Open Letter to the Christian Nobility of the German Nation Concerning the Reform of the Christian Estate, 1520) stated: 'No-one can do this so well as the temporal authorities, especially since now they are fellow Christians, fellow priests, fellow spirituals, fellow lords over all things and whenever it is needful or profitable, they should give free course to office and work in which God has put them above every man.'

However, with a complete reading of *1Peter 2:11-25* 'The Christian in the Hostile World' it is plain to see that St Peter is explaining that just as Christ Our Lord submitted Himself to the laws of man, so must the Christian. Just as Christ Our Lord held firmly to the will of God, living to the truth of God unto death, so must the Christian. The Christian under the law of man will suffer for doing good but that through the Christian, doing no evil or accepting no evil and only doing good, grace will abound. The Christian has to try to live free from sin, to live for righteousness so that like Christ Our Lord the Christian can become an example for all in the community. He does not say the Church is to be ruled by kings or governments. The danger when this happens, apart from the obvious theological ones, is that churches can then become nationalistic and church members can be drawn into a false pride because of race, which in turn may cause wars and holocausts to happen.

Clearly in the Word of God the apostolic authority and succession is set in place. Some, however, still question papal authority and do not believe in it. Yet, when St Peter, whose authority and primacy is clear in Holy Scripture, passed onto his successor his authority, his primacy, then this was 'bound in heaven and bound on earth.' If people choose not to believe this, it does not alter the fact that by the Word of God and by the authority of St Peter, his successors sit in his place and sit as leaders of Our Lord Jesus Christ's Holy Church.

Church and State

Governments all over the world today demand a separation of Church and state claiming the Church should have no influence on government policies and laws. Yet some of these same governments try and force their laws on the Church! Even in countries which were founded on Christian principles and by Christians, governments try to deny Christ.

The cry to separate Church and state is a humanist concept that dates back to ancient Greece and has spread like a cancer to many countries. No Christian should embrace humanism as it is in direct opposition to the truth of God. In humanism, usually there is no God, no soul, no after life and nothing supernatural. Humanism usually puts self first and living for the present…the here and now.

Of course it is important that the Church does not control governments, leaving people the freedom of choice, a God- given freedom. However, any politician who is Christian must in all things support Christian values and morals. Every Christian who votes must vote in support of Christ's way. This is a Christian duty. Not to do so is to deny Christ and in denying Christ allowing what may be un-Christian into their governments and into their lives *(Heb 3:12 Take care brothers that none of you may have an evil or unfaithful heart, so as to forsake the living God. Rom 14:22 Blessed is the one who does not condemn himself for what he approves).*

Christ Our Lord must come first in all things *(Eph 1:21 Far above every principality, authority, power and dominion. Col 1:17 He is before all things. Col 1:18 That in all things he himself might be preeminent. Col 2:10 Who is the head of every principality and power)*…this is the true Christian way.

Yes, the laws of governments should be obeyed and followed, except when they go against God's will,

Christ's will and the faith He gave to the world. If a law is immoral or is against the Word of God, Christian's must peacefully work to change those laws and certainly cannot accept those laws *(2 Tim 4:2 Proclaim the word; be persistent whether it is convenient or inconvenient, convince, reprimand, encourage through all patience and teaching)* and no argument that opposes the law of God can be accepted *(Eph 5:6 Let no one deceive you with empty arguments)*.

All Christians are called to stand for Christ, living in His way in their communities so that His loving peace and joy can fill the world making it a better place *(1 Corin 7:17 Everyone should live as the Lord has assigned, just as God called each one)*.

Church Scandals

In the Holy Apostolic Church there are people who at times do not live the way Christ Our Lord calls them to. The world often uses this to condemn the Church and to reject Christ Our Lord and His message. It is unfortunate that some do not see that because there are those in the Church who do not live right, it does not mean the Church is wrong or the message it proclaims of God's love is wrong. It only means people are weak and are prone to sin.

It has always been that way. St Peter sinned *(Mk 14:71 He began to curse and swear, 'I do not know this man about whom you are talking')*...he who was chosen to lead the Church! His sinning however did not stop the Lord Jesus loving him. Neither did it destroy or change the message of God's love or the authority Our Lord gave to him. It is the same for the Holy Apostolic Church. Yes, at times some within the Church will sin and sin terribly, but this does not destroy the authority or love of Christ in the Church *(Rom 3:2-4 In the first place they were entrusted with the utterances of God. What if some were unfaithful? Will their infidelity nullify the fidelity of God? Of course not!)*.

Here is a letter I published in 2003 in regard to a Church scandal:

Today, sadly the scandal of evil paedophilia is raising its ugly head within the Catholic Church. A number of priests have been found guilty of this heinous crime against children and this offense against the moral laws of God. It is right and justifiable that people within and outside the Church stand up and condemn these terrible acts so that those who have committed them can be brought to justice. It is also right to look at the processes that have allowed this to happen and to continue happening. Obviously there has been some lack of understanding in how to deal with these situations as they have occurred. We must pray that lessons have been learned from the past so that in future the correct actions are taken when facing this evil.

We as Church must also face up to the responsibility we have in caring for those innocents who have been hurt and do our best to help them through any difficulties they may have because of what they had to endure. We also now have to stand united against this evil which has entered the Church, for surely this is an attack of evil whose aim is to damage and break the Church. The perception now is that many priests are immoral and evil when in fact the vast majority are good and holy priests seeking to serve God and fellow man. It is in fact a very, very small minority of priest's who sin in such a way, yet, through the media, it appears as if this is commonplace among priests.

At present evil is launching a large attack on the good priests through the very few it has ensnared with sexual desires and deviations. Now is the time for all Catholics to support strongly and publicly their priests and not be drawn into the almost hysterical responses to what has happened. We must understand that in normal society a percentage of people behave in this terrible way but that does not mean all do. Priests are taken from society and so it is to be expected that a small percentage of them will have this sickness of evil within them but that does not mean all do. It does mean however that those seeking the priesthood must be scrutinized to a much greater degree than in the past, so that those with problems can be removed. We should realize too that these sick people in society will be drawn to vocations where children are placed in their care so that they can exploit this position. It does not only happen in the priesthood or only in the Catholic Church.

Today Catholics must be courageous in facing this threat to the Church not only courageous in helping root out this evil but also courageous in standing by their priests and proclaiming to the world that God in His love and mercy is working strongly in and through the priesthood. We must not let those who oppose the Church use this time to push their own agendas, i.e. married priests, women priests, homosexual priests, to name a few. Instead, we must be firm in our faith knowing that God will, with our cooperation, correct any wrongs in the Church and will, through the Church, bring His divine love to all.

We must not forget or ignore what has happened but we must forgive and we must stand with and in Christ to confront this evil which attacks His Church today.

Riches of the Church

The Holy Apostolic Church is often condemned over the wealth, the riches and the treasures it has. People ask why these are not used for the poor. The Church of course does help the poor through many missions; Mother Teresa's order is a fine example. In many poor countries the Church builds not only churches but hospitals and schools. The Church also has numerous programmes to help the poor with food, water, training for employment and much, much more.

Yet, some still ask why not sell all the Vatican treasures, not understanding that many are given in perpetuity to the Church, meaning it cannot sell them! Many are made or donated specifically for the Church and the glory of God to be seen within them, in the Church. Whole families, towns, villages or individuals have often sacrificed so that churches could be built or the Church could have these treasures to share with all people. Their intention was not that the Church should sell them but keep them. So then the Church rightly holds on to the treasures and passes them on to the future Church. The Church is a repository for these articles of faith, so that many can benefit from their spiritual beauty and not just a few wealthy private collectors around the world.

Personally, I have visited a very poor and run down church in need of extensive repair. There is an old painting hanging above the altar which is worth approximately $1,500,000. If they sold the painting this would solve all their financial problems but they cannot sell it as the painting was given in perpetuity.

It is to be remembered that the Roman Catholic Church never demands money or articles from people. Instead, it says give freely what you can, leaving up to each individual to decide. This is unlike some other denominations that demand a 'tithe' from their followers. Yet, who asks what do they do with the money or why isn't it used for the poor?

The Holy Apostolic Church must retain its treasures as they are there only in safekeeping. All those who think of this as greedy should remember the sacrifices the Church continuously makes around the world in lives, in holy work and in goods, reflecting on what treasures these are!

Sacraments

The Sacraments are efficacious signs of grace instituted by Christ and entrusted to the Church by which Divine life is dispensed to us (Catholic Catechism 1131).

There is disagreement amongst churches over the relevance, importance and the sacredness of the Sacraments. Some believe only in Baptism, while others believe in Baptism and the Eucharist, rejecting the other sacramental rites of the Holy Apostolic Church. With so many different views and beliefs it is important to look at the misunderstandings between people and to try and clarify them. It is not intended to explain the entirety of each sacrament because each one could fill a book. So this is just a brief reflection on the differences.

Baptism

When Adam first sinned in the Garden of Eden he condemned the souls of his descendants to be stained with original sin *(Rom 5:12 Therefore, just as through one person sin entered the world, and through sin, death, and thus death came to all, inasmuch as all sinned. 1 Corin 15:22 As in Adam all die).* However, God in His merciful love, gives mankind the grace in Him, by Baptism to have this stain removed *(Rom 5:18 Just as through one transgression condemnation came upon all so through one righteous act acquittal and life came to all).* In Baptism the person is buried into Christ's death from which they rise up by resurrection with Him as a new creature so that everyone can have the opportunity to enter heaven as a child of God *(Jn 3:5 Amen, Amen, I say to you no one can enter the kingdom of God without being born of water and spirit. Mk 16:16 Whoever believes and is baptized will be saved).*

Now some believe that Baptism should happen only when the person is no longer a child, so the person can make the decision for themselves. What a great danger this is because original sin remains on the soul weakening it and opening the soul to the attacks of evil. In Baptism, the original sin is removed as the Holy Spirit touches, purifies, justifies and sanctifies and so strengthens the soul making it less susceptible to the touches of evil it will face in life. *(Acts 2:38 Repent and be baptized, every one of you, in the name of Jesus Christ for forgiveness of your sins: and you will receive the gift of the holy spirit. 1 Corin 6:11 But now you have had yourself washed, you were sanctified, you were justified in the name of the Lord Jesus Christ and in the spirit of our God)* So to deny a child Baptism is to deny the gift of the Holy Spirit and deny the child coming to God.

Our Lord Jesus' words in Holy Scripture remind us not to keep the children from Him *(Mk 10:13 People were bringing the children to him that he might touch* them. *Mk 10:14 'Let the children come to me; do not prevent them, for the kingdom of God belongs to such as these.' Luke 18:15 People were bringing even infants to him).* There is an indication in the presentation of Our Lord as a baby in the temple when Joseph and Mary brought the Lord and presented Him to the Father in Heaven as His child, that we too should do the same being Christian imitators of Him.

Our Lord Jesus gave the Apostles authority to baptize *(Mt 28:19 Make disciples of all nations, baptizing them in the name of the Father and the Son and the holy Spirit).* Also in the Acts of the Apostles the authority to baptize was shown *(Acts 2:38)* at Pentecost when St Peter invited the crowd to be baptized and when St Paul baptized Lydia and her household *(Acts 16:15)* and later the jailer and his family *(Acts 16:33).* Also *(1 Corin 1:16 I baptized the household of Stephanus).* Baptism then is for all people of all ages but preferably as a child so that people can have this grace, this gift, of becoming a child of God with them to bring them to the fullness of life in Our Lord Jesus' love sooner rather than later.

Often people who were baptized when they were young, as they get older claim to have been baptized in the Holy Spirit or even born again when they attend various religious events. This of course cannot be, for once a person is completely baptized in Christ Our Lord they are baptized in the Holy Spirit *(Mt 28:19).* However, what may have happened now is that the person has the desire to live in the Holy Spirit and so removes the barriers of self and of life that have prevented the graces and gifts of the Holy Spirit coming alive within the person. (In the Latin Rite the completion of Baptism is confirmation.) So the person experiences what is already there but had been imprisoned before and now is being set free.

Once a person is baptized they are born in Christ Our Lord and cannot be born again *(Titus 3:5 Through the bath of rebirth and renewal by the holy Spirit).* What happens is that the person accepts what they may have denied or rejected before, that Jesus Christ is their Lord and Saviour. However, that was already true but now what occurs is that the scales fall from the person's eyes, from their spiritual sight and the person sees what already was true. These events, though mistitled, are very important because many people find through them the faith they may have lost or not known about. Many find the gifts and graces of the Holy Spirit strengthening their faith and the faith of others. Many find the joy of God's love for the first time in their lives and find His peace come into them.

Always though people should remember there is but one Baptism, it is a Sacrament given by God to mankind through His apostles and passed on through His Church. However, it is not only bishops, priests and deacons who can baptize but where it is a necessity any person can baptize if they have the required intention (Catholic Catechism 1256 - The intention required is to will to do what the Church does when she baptizes and to apply the Trinitarian baptismal formula).

Confirmation

Some believe the Sacrament of Confirmation is not necessary or not even a sacrament, believing that Baptism is all that is required to receive the gift of the Holy Spirit. However, in Holy Scripture it can be seen that it was after Our Lord was baptized the Holy Spirit descended upon Him. *(Mt 3:16 After Jesus was baptized, he came up from the water and behold the heavens were opened for him and he saw the Spirit of God descending like a dove and coming upon him. Mk, 1:10 On coming up out of the water he saw the heavens being torn open and the Spirit, like a dove, descending upon him. Luke 3: 21-22 After all the people had been baptized and Jesus also had been baptized and was praying, heaven was opened and the holy Spirit descended upon him in bodily form like a dove)* Also, that some disciples had been baptized but did not receive the Holy Spirit until the laying on of hands *(Acts 19:2-3 Did you receive the holy spirit when you became believers? They answered him, 'We have never even heard that there is a holy Spirit.' He said, 'How were you baptized?' They replied, 'With the baptism of John.' Acts 19:6 And when Paul laid his hands on them, the holy Spirit came upon them. Acts 8:14-17 They sent Peter and John, who went down and prayed for them, that they might receive the holy Spirit, for it had not yet fallen on any of them, they had only been baptized in the name of the Lord Jesus. Then they laid hands on them and they received the Holy Spirit).*

In Hebrews Baptism and the laying on of hands are mentioned as two separate things but mentioned with the same importance *(Heb 6:2 Instruction about baptisms and laying on of hands)* so if Baptism is accepted as a sacrament so too must be the laying on of hands in the receiving of the Holy Spirit. There are two traditions in the Holy Apostolic Church, east and west. In the Eastern Church Confirmation is administered immediately after Baptism by the priest but he can only do so with the perfumed oil (Myron) 'Chrism' consecrated by a bishop. In the Latin Church this sacrament is administered when the age of reason has been reached and its celebration is ordinarily reserved for the bishop.

Confirmation, a sacrament in its own right, as shown in Holy Scripture, which perfects and completes baptismal grace. Confirmation brings the Holy Spirit to the person so that each one can have a deeper, more intimate relationship with the Father and the Son and the Holy Spirit. Confirmation, by the grace and gift of the Holy Spirit, strengthens a person to live and bear witness to Christ Our Lord so that His love, through His Church, through His people can reach out and change the world.

The Eucharist

Of all the sacraments the Eucharist is the greatest, for it is in the Eucharist people can become one with and in God. It is in the Eucharist that God lowers Himself to come into sinful human beings. It is in the Eucharist the bread and wine become the body and blood of Our Lord Jesus *(Luke 22:19 This is my body. Luke 22:20 This cup is the new covenant in my blood. Mt 26:26 This is my body. Mt 26:27 For this is my blood. Mark 14:22 This is my body. Mark 14:24 This is my blood).*

Yet among the Christian churches are an array of beliefs ranging from a total belief of the presence of the Lord in the Eucharist which remains until the body and blood is consumed, to a total denial of Christ Our Lord's presence in the bread and wine.

To look at Our Lord's words in Holy Scripture should clarify what the truth is. In the Gospel of St John Our Lord tells mankind He is the bread of life and that if people want to live eternally they must eat of Him *(Jn 6:48-51 I am the bread of life. Your ancestors ate the manna in the desert, but they died; this is the bread that comes down from heaven so that one may eat it and not die. I am the living bread that came down from heaven, whoever eats of this bread will live forever and the bread that I shall give is my flesh for the life of the world).* Among the Jews some found this hard to accept so the Lord confirmed it *(Jn 6:53-56 Jesus said to them, 'Amen, Amen, I say to you, unless you eat the flesh of the Son of Man and drink his blood, you do not have life within you. Whoever eats my flesh and drinks my blood has eternal life and I will raise him on the last day. For my flesh is true food and my blood is true drink. Whoever eats my flesh and drinks my blood remains in me and I in him').*

The Lord also stated that to remain in Him and for Our Lord to remain in us, we must eat and drink of

His divine body and blood. Many, however, find it hard to accept these holy words, while some deny these holy words completely just as many of the Jews did when Our Lord declared this divine mystery to mankind *(Jn 6:60 This saying is hard, who can accept it?)*. Our Lord was aware that people would reject, deny or not understand His holy words *(Jn 6:63-64 'The words I have spoken to you are spirit and life. But there are some of you who do not believe.' Jesus knew from the beginning the ones who would not believe)* but He did not change His words even though many by their own free will turned away from Him *(Jn 6:66 As a result of this many of his disciples returned to their former way of life)*.

Later at the Last Supper Our Lord showed mankind what is His body and blood that all are called to eat of *(Mt 26:26-28 Jesus took the bread, said the blessing, broke it and giving it to his disciples said, 'Take and eat this is my body.' Then he took a cup, gave thanks and gave it to them saying, 'Drink from it all of you for this is my blood'). (Mk 14:22-24. Luke 22:19-20)*.

It was at the Last Supper the Lord also gave the command to do this *(Luke 22:19 'Do this in memory of me')*. This command calls all who love Our Lord Jesus Christ to come to Him in the Eucharist. He also commands His Church to continue the Eucharistic celebration which the early Church did in obedience to His will *(Acts 2:42 They devoted themselves to the teaching of the apostles and to the communal life, to the breaking of the bread and to the prayers. Acts 20:7 On the first day of the week we gathered to break bread)*.

There are those who believe this is and should be only a symbolic act, yet, Our Lord did not say it was to be symbolic He told all who would listen they must eat and drink of Him. He then gave us Himself in the Eucharist so that we would know where to go to receive the divine body and blood. His early Church continued to do as He said. Later St Paul reminded the Corinthians of the truth of the Eucharist *(1 Corin 10:16 The cup of blessing that we bless is it not a participation in the blood of Christ? The bread that we break, is it not a participation in the body of Christ?)*. Nothing symbolic here! St Paul also states again the command the Lord gave *(1Corin 11:24 'Do this in remembrance of me')* and gives a grave warning *(1Corin 11:27 'Therefore whoever eats the bread or drinks the cup of the Lord unworthily will have to answer for the body and blood of the Lord')*. Why would St Paul give such a warning if it was only a symbolic act? He gives it because, as he proclaims, it is <u>the body and the blood</u> of the Lord. St Paul is also confirming that God, through His Holy Church, through His ministers, changes the bread and wine into the body and blood of Our Lord Jesus, therefore the church is obeying the command that was given.

Some denominations believe that Christ Our Lord is truly present but only in the Eucharistic celebration and during the Eucharistic celebration. However, nowhere does Our Lord say that this is His body and blood only for a short time or this is His body and blood until people believe it changes back to bread and wine. Once the bread and wine is changed into the body and blood of Jesus it remains so until it is consumed. It is in the eating of the Lord that His body and blood becomes part of the person, bringing the person to oneness in Him and to union with Christ and so His divine presence, which cannot be destroyed or removed, is now alive within the person and the person is now alive in Christ.

Others doubt in Jesus' presence, as I used to, because they see only bread and wine before them and truly do not believe that the priests or even God has the power to change it. What I, and others forgot or forget, is that God is all powerful *(Luke 1:37 For nothing will be impossible to God)*. He has made the universe, all of creation, you and me. So if God, through the priests, who are keeping the Lord's Command, wants to change the bread and wine into the body, blood, soul and divinity of His Son Jesus, He can and He does by the power of His Holy Spirit *(Jn 14:15-17 'If you love me you will keep my commandments, and I will ask the Father and he will give you another advocate to be with you always, the spirit of truth.')*.

God in His mercy gives mankind physical food to sustain and strengthen peoples' bodies and as God cares also for souls He too gives the spiritual food that is needed to nourish souls so that the soul, the spirit, the entire human being can find fullness of life in Him. It is when the Lord is received within at the Eucharist that His body, His blood, His soul, His divinity, fills the person and when the person, in faith, gives themselves to Christ in the Eucharist, that the entire being is then immersed in Our Divine Lord and changes in Him to be more like Him. It is in this greatest of the Sacraments that fullness of life, fullness of faith can be found because in receiving the divine presence of Jesus Christ Our Lord people are filled with life *(Jn 6:57 'Who feeds on me will have life')* and can find the strength to live the faith Our Lord calls each one to.

It is in and through the Eucharist people can truly become Christ-like, as Christ Our Lord will be within the person filling them with the grace to live the way He calls everyone to live, to live the Christian life as the light of Christ to the world.

Reconciliation

There are substantial disagreements over the need for Reconciliation with some seeing it as unnecessary because they can go directly to God and therefore do not need the Sacrament, saying it is only God who can forgive sins and not the Church, not the priests. Yet, Our Lord, in Holy Scripture after showing He had the power to forgive sins *(Mt 9:2-6 "Courage child your sins are forgiven." "But that you may know the Son of Man has authority on earth to forgive sins")* also confirmed His Apostolic Church would by God's authority and grace be able to do so in His name *(Mt 9:8 They were struck with awe and glorified God who had given such authority to human beings. Jn 20:22-23 He breathed on them and said, "Receive the holy Spirit whose sins you forgive are forgiven them and whose sins you retain are retained.")*. So in the living and Holy Word of God, the Lord passed on His power to forgive to His chosen ones which St Paul confirmed in his letter to the Corinthians *(2 Corin 5:18 And all this is from God, who has reconciled us to himself through Christ and given us the ministry of reconciliation)*. St James also writes on the Sacrament of Reconciliation *(James 5:15-16 If he has committed any sins he will be forgiven. Therefore confess your sins to one another and pray for one another that you may be healed)*.

Today many people profess to live to the Word of God but somehow find reasons not to accept some of what God says to us. A common statement is that in the 'Our Father' we ask God for forgiveness and that is enough. In the 'Our Father' the Lord is showing people, yes, we must come to God seeking forgiveness but in His Holy Word He directs us to come to God through those He in His wisdom chose to dispense this grace. It is important to understand that the priest is forgiving sins by the power and grace of the Holy Spirit *(Jn 20:22-23)*. So it is not the humanity of the priest forgiving sins but the Divinity of God through the humanity of the priest that does so. It also follows that if St Peter or any of his successors said that people are to come to Reconciliation and confess their sins and that only the priests in the Sacrament have the power, by the grace of God to forgive sins, then this is by Jesus' Word bound in heaven and on earth.

Others say that in their proclaiming Jesus Christ as their Lord and Saviour and by clinging to the cross, that His sacrifice covers and forgives their past, present and future sins. This may be true but what is also true is that when a person proclaims Jesus as Lord and gives themselves to Him in a Christian life the person must repent of their sins and try their best not to sin again *(Jn 8:11 From now on do not sin any more)*. In the act of repentance a person is called by Christ to confess their sins and to confess them to those Our Lord gave the authority to forgive. If this was not so, why then did God give this power to man? There would be no point to it and as all who love God know, there is always a point to His Divine Word.

In this proclamation of Jesus Christ as Lord and Saviour every person is called to live a life aiming at perfection in Christ Our Lord *(Heb 5:9 He was made perfect. Mt 5:48 So be perfect, just as your heavenly Father is perfect)*. The Sacrament of Reconciliation is here to help people to do so, because with frequent Reconciliation people look at their mistakes, turn to God, confess their sins and are forgiven them. Then given a cleansing, a healing, a strengthening of their soul, so that it will become easier to walk the right way in avoiding sin, in avoiding mistakes. The grace of the Sacrament of Reconciliation takes away the blindness of worldly and self centered sight and offers a clearer spiritual sight to all. When the stain of sin is removed from the soul the darkness that clouds peoples' sight is dispersed by the divine light of the Holy Spirit that pours out through the priest and into the person. Then the right way to walk in life becomes more obvious and the traps and lures of evil lose their attraction. No wonder evil tries to confuse people so that they will not believe in and accept what God offers in the holy Sacrament of Reconciliation, what God has given people and directed people to in His Holy Word.

There is also a grave misunderstanding that leads some to believe that it is God who causes sin and so there is no need to confess it. Martin Luther believed human nature had been totally corrupted by original sin and because of this mankind had been deprived of free will. Whatever people do, good or bad, is not their own work but God's. This then would mean that God does bad work, that God sins. Yet, this is impossible, for God is pure love where no sin resides. God is perfection itself *(Mt 5:48 Your heavenly Father is perfect)* and so there cannot be the flaw of evil or sin in God *(Heb 4:15 Without sin)*. What this may cause people to believe is that they have little responsibility for their sins as it is God's will, not theirs. With this anyone who sins, regardless of how great the sin, can say it is God's work and can believe to continue sinning is acceptable. Yet in Holy Scripture we are clearly told this is not so *(Sirach 15:11-13 Say not, 'It was God's doing that I fell away' for what he hates he does not do. Say not, 'It was he who set me astray,' for he has no need of wicked man. Abominable wickedness the Lord hates)* and in respect to free will *(Sirach 15:14-15 When God in the beginning, created man, he made him subject to his own free choice. If you choose you can keep the commandments; it is loyalty to do his will)*.

Martin Luther, in his letter to Melancthon, (Letter No 99, 1st August 1521, 'Let Your Sins Be Strong') states: 'Be a sinner, and let your sins be strong - no sin can separate us from him, even if we were to kill or commit adultery thousands of times each day.' And to Enders ('Briefwechsel' III 208) 'Be a sinner and sin on bravely, but have stronger faith and rejoice in Christ, who is the victor of sin, death and the world. Do not for a moment imagine that this life is the abiding place of justice. Sin must be committed. To you it ought to be sufficient that you acknowledge the lamb that takes away the sins of the world, the sin cannot tear you away from him, even though you commit adultery a hundred times a day and commit as many murders.'

These statements suggest it is alright to sin and to break the Commandments as long as you cling to Jesus' sacrifice and call Him Lord. Yet Our Lord said not to sin or break the Commandments *(Jn 8:11 From now on do not sin anymore. Jn 14:15 If you love me you will keep my Commandments).* The Lord also very clearly told people that to call Him 'Lord' yet to continue to do wrong will not bring some to His kingdom *(Mt 7:21-23 'Not everyone who says to me, 'Lord, Lord,' will enter the kingdom of heaven, but only the one who does the will of my Father in heaven. Many will say to me on that day, 'Lord, Lord, did we not prophesy in your name? Did we not drive out demons in your name? Did we not do mighty deeds in your name?' Then I will declare to them solemnly, 'I never knew you, depart from me, you evildoers." Luke 6:46 'Why do you call me 'Lord, Lord,' but do not do what I command?' Luke 13:26-27 And you will say, 'We ate and drank in your company and you taught in our streets.' Then he will say to you, 'I do not know where you are from. Depart from me, all you evildoers.').*

Here Our Lord says it is not enough to call Him Lord and to cling to Him and to do His work if you do not live to God's commandments *(Mt 19:17-19 If you wish to enter into life keep the commandments. He asked him, 'Which ones?' And Jesus replied, 'You shall not kill; you shall not commit adultery; you shall not steal; you shall not bear false witness; honour your father and your mother; and you shall love your neighbour as yourself.' Mk 10:19-20).*

While Our Lord confirms that sin will be committed, there is also stated the danger of sinning *(Mt 18:7 'Woe to the one through whom they come.')*. Sin does tear us away from Christ Our Lord because in sinning, regardless of the reason, people reject the Commandments and deny the Divine Word of Jesus Our Lord; deny the love of Christ. *(Jn 14:15 If you love me you will keep my commandments. 1 Jn 2:4 Whoever says, 'I know him,' but does not keep his commandments is a liar and the truth is not in him. 1 Jn 3:4-6 Everyone who commits sin commits lawlessness for sin is lawlessness-no one who remains in him sins; no one who sins has seen him or known him. 1 Corin 6:9-10 Do you not know the unjust will not inherit the kingdom of God. Nor adulterers will inherit the kingdom of God).*

In sinning, people push the cross away from them, instead of placing themselves with Christ Our Lord on the cross and seeking the power of His sacrifice to overcome sin in their lives. It is sin, that in the beginning separated man from God and it is sin that continues to do so, unless people repent and come to the cross for the strength needed to try and live the right way *(Rom 6:1 Shall we persist in sin that grace may abound, of course not)*. For those who love Christ Our Lord, sin becomes abhorrent. The knowledge that sin offends Our Lord makes a desire not to sin strong in the hearts of those who love Him and so a natural part of that true love is to reject all sin.

Predestination

People sometimes believe certain ones are chosen, predestined to be with God in heaven. That whatever happens in life, God has already set in place and this will happen, regardless of what people do. So if someone sins it was predestined and why then does a person need to confess? Surely a person could behave as they wanted and their destiny would not be affected by their behaviour.

However, God gives people choices in this life, *(Sirach 15:14 He made him subject to his own free choice)* choices that can lead to heaven or hell. Why would God give choice if all were predestined? This is an immense sign of God's love for mankind, that He gives this freedom. If there were predestination why would Our Lord Jesus have come to encourage us to live good and holy lives, for it would not matter! If there was predestination that would mean God loves some people more than others. Yet His words tell people that He loves everyone and that salvation is there for all those who will embrace His love and forgiveness.

Predestination is a misunderstanding of God's merciful love and a rejection of His act of salvation for all on the cross. Predestination is just another excuse to justify sin *(Heb 10:26-27 If we sin deliberately after receiving knowledge of the truth, there no longer remains sacrifice for sins but a fearful prospect of judgement and a flaming fire)*.

Anointing of the Sick

Most people recognize the healing power of Christ Our Lord when He walked the earth, which is mentioned numerous times in Holy Scripture. Most Christians today believe that Our Lord passed on His healing power through the apostles to the Church *(Mk 16:18 They will lay lands on the sick and they will recover. Mt 10:8 Cure the sick)* and that many today heal in the name of Jesus because of the Lord's instructions to the apostles and His giving of the healing power to them *(Mark 6:13 They drove out demons, and anointed with oil many who were sick and cured them. Acts 3:7 Then Peter took him by the right hand and raised him up and immediately his feet and hands grew strong. Acts 5:15 Thus they even carried the sick out into the streets and lay them on cots and mats so that when Peter came by, at least his shadow might fall on one or another of them. Acts 5:16 Bringing the sick and those disturbed by unclean spirits and they were all cured)*.

There is, however, some disagreement over the 'Sacrament of the Sick' as some believe healing is a gift and not a sacrament. Yet Christ Our Lord healed and commanded the apostles and through them the Church to heal *(Mt 10:8 Cure the sick)* so making the healing power of the church sacred, a sacrament. Yes, the Holy Spirit does give some people a special gift of healing through prayer, a charismatic gift, but this is different to the sacramental healing Christ Our Lord also calls for in His command to the Church.

This Sacrament is of course dispensed by the priests, often it is celebrated within the Eucharist and it involves anointing the sick with holy oil blessed by the bishop or if necessary the priest himself, as directed by St James in Holy Scripture *(James 5:14 Is anyone among you sick? He should summon the presbyters of the church and they should pray over him and anoint him with oil in the name of the Lord)* and as practiced by the apostles when the Lord sent them on their mission, which today is the mission of the Holy Apostolic Church *(Mk 6:13 They anointed with oil many who were sick and cured them).* Every time a Christian has a serious illness they may receive the 'Sacrament of the Sick' and also if after they have received it, the illness becomes worse.

The 'Sacrament of the Sick' differs therefore from the charism of healing that some possess because of the Command and authority Our Lord, Jesus gave to the apostles and Church. In the charism of healing it is an individual or a group of people praying to the Lord for healing. Maybe calling on the Father, calling on the name of Jesus, calling on the Holy Spirit to work through them to pour out His healing power and to cure the person. While in the 'Sacrament of the Sick' it is the Church with the authority of Christ Our Lord, through the priest, blessing and anointing the sick as commanded by God. It is the Church fulfilling what Our Lord asks and it is Christ in His body the Church, touching the sick with His holy anointing, with His Holy Spirit.

The charism of healing is a great blessing where God works through people to heal others. An even greater blessing is 'The anointing of the sick' where Our Lord Himself in His body, the Church, pours out His sacred healing power, His Divine grace and His Divine mercy.

Holy Orders

The priesthood for many years has been subject to frequent attacks, some of which deny the priesthood, some of which try to change the priesthood and some of which try to destroy the priesthood.

Looking to Holy Scripture it can be seen there are several confirmations of the appointment of priests *(Acts 6:3 Brothers select from among you seven reputable men, filled with the spirit and wisdom, whom we shall appoint to the task. Acts 6:6 They presented these men to the apostles who prayed and laid hands on them. Acts 13:1-3 Now there were in the church of Antioch prophets and teachers-the holy spirit said, 'Set apart Barnabas and Saul for the work to which I have called them,' then completing their fasting and prayers they laid hands on them and sent them off. Acts 14:23 They appointed presbyters for them in each church. Acts 20:17 He had the presbyters of the church Ephesus summoned. Acts 20:28 Keep watch over yourselves and over the whole flock of which the holy Spirit has appointed you overseers, in which you tend the church of God. 1 Tim 4:14 The gift you have which was conferred on you through the prophetic word with the imposition of hands of this presbyterate. 2 Tim 1:6 The gift of God you have through the imposition of my hands. Titus 1:5 Appoint presbyters in every town as I directed you).* These show the priests (presbyters) are appointed by the apostles and Church hierarchy with the laying on of hands and directed to watch over the flock, to tend the Church. The priests are chosen from good men within the Church and presented for the laying on of hands.

The Holy Scripture references also answer some of the major questions and misunderstandings about the priesthood.

Are all Priests?

Martin Luther, in 'An Open Letter to the Christian Nobility of the German Nation,' states through Baptism all of us are consecrated to the priesthood *(1 Peter 2:9 'Ye are a royal priesthood, a priestly kingdom.' Rev 5:10 'Thou hast made us by thy blood to be priests and kings')*. Luther also states, 'The whole congregation, all of whom have like-power, were to take one out of their number and charge him to use this power for the others.' From this it follows there is no difference between laymen and priests, princes and bishops 'spirituals' and 'temporals,' as they call them. Yes, it is true that by Baptism the whole Church is a priestly people, that all share in the priesthood of Christ called the common priesthood. However, the New Testament shows there are those chosen and called from the common priesthood to the sacred ministry of the priest just as in the Old Testament where the chosen people were made by God *(Ex 19:6 A kingdom of priests and a holy nation)*. But from within them God chose Aaron and his sons, then the tribe of Levi to be priests *(Ex 28:1 From among the Israelites have your brother Aaron, together with his sons Nadab, Abihu, Eleazar and Ithamar brought to you, that they may be my priests. Ex 29:1 This is the rite you shall perform in consecrating them priests)*.

The Holy Spirit said to *(Acts 13:2 'Set apart Barnabas and Saul for the work that I have called them.' Acts 6:3 'Select from among you seven reputable men.')*. Also it is clear that it is not the common priesthood that appoints the priest but the apostles and their successors (bishops) by the laying on of hands *(Acts 6:3 'Whom we (the apostles) shall appoint.' Acts 14:23 'They appointed presbyters for them in each church. Titus 1:5 'Appoint presbyters in every town, as I directed you.')*.

It is also evident that the priests are there to watch over and guide the Church and are appointed by the

Holy Spirit to do so *(Acts 20:17, 20:28).* Luther also states, 'Therefore a priest in office is nothing more than an office holder. When in office he has a precedence; when deposed, he is a peasant or a townsman like the rest. Beyond all doubt, then, a priest is no longer a priest.' Yet, in Holy Scripture it says a priest is a priest forever *(Heb 5:6, Heb 7:17 You are a priest forever in the order of Melchizedek. Ex 29:9 Thus shall the priesthood be theirs by perpetual law).* Luther also states 'But that a pope or a bishop anoints, confers tonsures; ordains, consecrates, or prescribes dress unlike that of the laity, this may make hypocrites and graven images.'

However, God in His Divine wisdom says that when the priests are consecrated they should be clothed in a special way *(Ex 29:5-6 Take the vestments and clothe Aaron with the tunic, the robe of the ephod, the ephod itself, and the breastpiece, fastening the embroidered belt of the ephod around him. Put the miter on his head, the sacred diadem on the miter. Ex 29:8-9 Bring forward his sons also and clothe them with the tunics, gird them with the sashes and tie the turbans on them. Thus shall the priesthood be theirs by perpetual law and thus shall you ordain Aaron and his sons).*

Once again, from Holy Scripture the priesthood is confirmed and the selection of men consecrated to be priests, to be set aside to serve God's Church in this special and holy ministry.

Homosexuality and the Priesthood

There are churches today that claim the ordination of homosexual priests and even the elevation of a homosexual to the bishopric is morally and faithfully correct. This by Holy Scripture, by the Word of God, is not so *(Acts 6:3 Brothers select from among you seven reputable men, filled with the spirit and wisdom).* To be reputable, spirit-filled and wise means a person must try not to sin and to live the Christian life.

It is clear that homosexuality is not God's way, is not Christ's way but is a sinful way *(Gn 18:20 The outcry against Sodom and Gomorrah is so great, and their sin so grave. Lev 18:22 You shall not lie with a male as with a woman; such a thing is an abomination. Lev 20:13 If a man lies with a male as with a woman, both of them shall be put to death for their abominable deed. Rom 1:26-27 Their females exchanged natural relations for unnatural and the males likewise gave up natural relations with females and burned with lust for one another. Males did shameful things with males. - 1 Corin 6:9 Do not be deceived; Neither fornicators nor idolaters nor adulterers nor boy prostitutes nor practicing homosexuals. 1 Corin 6:10 Will inherit the kingdom of God. - 1 Tim 1:9 The godless and sinful, the unholy and profane. 1 Tim 1:10 Practicing homosexuals).*

From this it is abundantly clear that no homosexual can rightly be ordained to the priesthood. People must of course remember not to judge nor condemn those with homosexual tendencies. Often people do not choose to be this way. Homosexuals should be treated with respect, compassion, love and should be given all the help and encouragement needed to come to terms with their condition, to control it and to lead a chaste life and if possible to overcome their condition. While it is essential there is no discrimination against homosexuals, it is also essential and correct and confirmed by God's Holy Word that no homosexual should be ordained a priest.

Women Priests and Women's Role in the Church

In recent times, in various denominations, women have been ordained priests and in many of the churches there is some support for this. Again, it is important to look at how God set the priesthood in place. In the Old Testament men were chosen for the priesthood. When Christ Our Lord, the High Priest, came to earth He came as a man. Those Our Lord chose to be apostles and to whom He passed on authority were men. At the Last Supper, the first Eucharist, Our Lord did not invite His Mother Mary, Mary Magdala or any other of His female followers who were in Jerusalem at the time. Our Lord only invited the apostles and passed onto and through them the celebration of the 'Sacrament of the Sacraments,' the Eucharist. Later, when the apostles ordained priests it was only men they ordained. So God in His wisdom and for His reasons chose men for the priesthood and who is anyone to change that? Therefore the Holy Apostolic Church is bound by Christ's choice and cannot alter it. Some see this as an oppression of women within the Church but it is not, it is just the following of God's will instead of the world's will.

This, however, does not mean God loves men more than women. In His eyes men and women are equal but also in His will men and women have different roles to fulfil. In no way does this detract from women, as it was a woman God first filled with His body, His blood, His soul, His divinity...Himself, when He entered Our Blessed Mother Mary in a unique way. No man has ever had such a relationship with God or such a privilege from God, nor can they ever.

Women, loved by God the same as men and in His love given a beautiful and blessed role to play within the Church and within the world. This can be seen by the great number of female saints proclaimed by the

Church and the holy women declared Doctors of the Church. Women's roles...different to men's but of equal value...roles all who love God should accept and respect.

Married Priests

At present there is a great debate over married priests and their role in the Church. Martin Luther in 'Let Your Sins Be Strong,' states that priests should be allowed to marry and that it is the devil that stops them doing so *(1 Tim 4:1-3 Forbidding marriage is a demonic instruction).* Others also quote *(1 Tim 3:2 Bishop must be married only once).*

There are two different disciplines followed in the Holy Apostolic Church. In the eastern Churches, while bishops are chosen only from celibate priests, married men can become deacons or priests. However, a man who has already been ordained as a priest cannot marry. Interestingly, celibate priesthood is highly esteemed and many priests choose to be celibate. In the western Church, the Latin Church, usually ordained priests are celibate. Those who seek the priesthood are aware of this commitment to God and freely make this vow, this promise to God and the Church. Like all vows before God it is one that should not be broken *(1 Tim 5:11-12 They want to marry and will incur condemnation for breaking their first pledge).* The Latin Church asks for celibacy taking its guidance from Holy Scripture (*Mt 19:12 Some, because they have renounced marriage for the sake of the kingdom of heaven, whoever can accept this ought to accept it. 1 Corin 7:8 Now to the unmarried and to widows I say: It is a good thing for them to remain as they are, as I do. 1 Corin 7:32 I should like you to be free of anxieties, an unmarried man is anxious about the things of the Lord, how he may please the Lord. 1 Corin 7:35 I am telling you this for your own benefit, not to impose a restraint upon you but for the sake of propriety and adherence to the Lord without distraction. 1 Corin 7:37 The one who stands firm in his resolve, however, who is not under compulsion but has power over his own will, and has made up his mind to keep his virgin will be doing well. 2 Tim 2:3-4 Bear your share of hardship along with me like a good soldier of Christ Jesus. To satisfy the one who recruited him, a soldier does not become entangled in business affairs of life).*

Some believe the Catholic Church forces this upon priests but everyone who believes this should remember that the Catholic Church forces no one to be a priest. Men freely choose to be priests knowing what is expected of them. While for some priests the vow of celibacy may be hard, it is important to remember the sacrifice that is made in celibacy is a sharing in the sacrifice of the Lord. That when, through the hardship that may come with celibacy, the priest clings to Christ Our Lord on the cross and endures this hardship in love of Christ, the priest opens himself to divine grace in a special way which can lift him to higher spiritual levels. Then through the priest the flock he shepherds will also be drawn to a deeper spirituality and opened to more grace.

It is by fulfilling this vow the priest shows obedience to the body of Christ, the Church. It is by rejecting this vow the priest shows disobedience to the Church and to the authority invested in it by Christ Our Lord. It is evident in Holy Scripture that celibacy is encouraged by Our Lord and the apostles, that it is not from the devil. It is also true that the Church forces no one to live the celibate life, it only insists those who by their own choice have made this promise to God, keep it.

One of the arguments in support of married priests is that there would be more priests and that congregations would increase in numbers. However, the Anglican Church in the U.K., which has married priests, homosexual priests and women priests by its own figures disprove this. The 'Daily Telegraph' dated 6/12/03 published a church report mentioning amongst other things the church's falling numbers and also showing less Anglican priests in 2003 than in 1902. In 1902 there were 31 bishops, 22 suffragens and 23,670 clergy, a total of 23,723. In 2003 44 bishops, 69 suffragens and 17,700 clergy, a total of 17,813. By these figures it seems neither married, nor homosexual, nor women priests have increased priestly or congregational numbers!

Marriage

The sacrament of marriage is in the world today under constant attack. Many now openly declare there is no reason for marriage. Many see marriage only as a temporal institution. Many see marriage as something that can be broken and that can be participated in more than once; some reports claim that approximately two out of every five marriages end in divorce. Today many Christians deny and reject the wonderful gift of love God offers to a man and woman in marriage, even at times declaring in the name of God that homosexual marriages are acceptable.

Marriage is a God-given institution which from the very beginning God gave so that man and woman could unite and become one *(Gn 2:24 That is why man leaves his father and mother and clings to his wife and the two of them become one body).* In the beginning God showed marriage was for man and woman *(Gn 2:18 I will make a suitable partner for him)* when He made woman as the suitable partner for man.

(Gn 1:27 Male and female he created them). In this the Lord plainly showed it was not to be man and man or

woman and woman united in marriage but a sacred and divinely instituted union of man and woman *(Mal 2:14 Because the Lord is witness between you and the wife of your youth).*

Our Lord in the New Testament confirmed the sacredness of marriage by His coming into the family of Joseph and Mary who were husband and wife. He did not come to a single man or a single woman or into a homosexual relationship. In His Holy Word He explained the divine will for marriage *(Mt 19:4-7 and Mk 10:6-9 The creator made them male and female- and the two shall become one flesh. So they are no longer two but one flesh. Therefore what God has joined together, no human being must separate).* Interestingly, the first public miracle Our Lord performed was at the wedding feast of Cana *(Jn 2:1-12).*

So it becomes obvious now how sacred marriage is in God's eyes and how it should be a sacred institution in the world as well. St Paul also directs people on marriage *(1 Corin 7:2 Every man should have his own wife and every woman her own husband. 1 Corin 7:36 Let them get married. 1 Corin 7:38 So then the one who marries his virgin does well. Eph 5:33 In any case each one of you should love his wife as himself and the wife should respect her husband. 1 Thess 4:3-4 This is the will of God; your holiness; that you refrain from immorality, that each of you know how to acquire a wife for himself in holiness and honour).* Holy Scripture confirms marriage is not only a temporal institution but a spiritual celebration given by God. That marriage unites man and woman not only in a physical but also in a spiritual way *(Eph 5:22-32)*, that the union of man and woman in marriage is an image of Our Lord Jesus and the Church. So that both unite to become one in God's eyes *(Mal 2:15 Did he not make one being with flesh and spirit).*

In the holy union of marriage each person is called to sacrifice for the other *(Eph 5:21 Be subordinate to one another out of reverence for Christ)* seeing that it is through the sacrifice of love that a marriage can grow. The sacrifice of love by Christ Our Lord on the cross, who carries all people's pain, hurt, frustrations and sufferings. As well by the sacrifice of love a husband or a wife makes one for the other *(Eph 5:24 Husbands, love your wives, even as Christ loved the church and handed himself over for her)*. So in marriage people can in a special way unite in the sacrificial love of Our Lord Jesus by turning to Him on the cross and offering Him all their difficulties and asking Him for the grace to overcome them. It is in doing this that not only do the man and woman become one in each other but now too they become one in the love of Christ; one in His sacrificial love.

Some men and women reject marriage and live together in 'de facto' relationships. This opposes God's will as seen in Holy Scripture where even *(Rev 19:7 'The wedding day of the lamb has come')* Christ wedded to the Church is proclaimed. Living together is in opposition to the morals God has given to mankind, making a 'de facto' or a 'living together relationship' immoral *(1 Corin 6:18 Avoid immorality. Every other sin a person commits is outside the body, but the immoral person sins against his own body. 1 Thess 4:3-5 This is the will of God, your holiness; that you refrain from immorality, that each of you know how to acquire a wife for himself in holiness and honour, not in lustful passion as do the gentiles who do not know God. 1 Thess 4:7-8 For God did not call us to impurity but to holiness. Therefore whoever disregards this, disregards not a human being but God. Eph 5:3 Immorality or any impurity or greed must not even be mentioned among you. Eph 5:5 Be sure of this, that no immoral or impure or greedy person, that is, an idolater has any inheritance in the kingdom of Christ and of God)*. It is suggested that if people live together in a trial relationship before they marry divorce will be less likely but the increased number of divorces uncover the great deception in this argument.

It is not an uncommon practice today for Christians to get divorced and remarried which again is the way of the world and not the way of God *(Mal 2:16 For I hate divorce, says the Lord, the God of Israel).* As the world attacks marriage, divorce, which was rejected by most Christians in the past, is now seen as acceptable by many. Yet, Christ Our Lord, spoke so plainly about divorce *(Mt 5:31 It was also said 'Whoever divorces his wife must give her a bill of divorce. But I say to you whoever divorces his wife (unless the marriage is unlawful) causes her to commit adultery and whoever marries a divorced woman commits adultery.' Mt 19:9 I say to you, whoever divorces his wife (unless the marriage is unlawful) and marries another commits adultery. Mk 10:11-12 He said to them 'Whoever divorces his wife and marries another commits adultery against her; and if she divorces her husband and marries another, she commits adultery.' Luke 16:18 Everyone who divorces his wife and marries another commits adultery and the one who marries a woman divorced from her husband commits adultery).*

However, it seems many ignore God's desire for people to keep marriage sacred and not to divorce. Obviously St Paul faced similar problems and so stated *(1 Corin 7:27 Are you bound to a wife? Do not seek separation).* Marriage by the Word of God then cannot be broken unless it is unlawful.

In the case of unlawful marriages the Church grants annulments and the people are then free to marry. However Pope John Paul II, warned, when speaking to members of the Roman Rota, that Church marriage tribunals should avoid an overly loose interpretation of a provision allowing annulments because of either spouse's 'incapacity for consent' to marriage (CNS). In some cases though it is impossible for people to stay together even though married. If this is so, people can physically separate but are still married in the eyes of God. So they are not free to start another sexual relationship, another union and must, even though living apart, keep living as a married person *(1 Corin 7:10-11 To the married, however, I give this instruction (not I, but the Lord): a wife should not separate from her husband-and if she does separate she must either remain single or become reconciled to her husband-and a husband should not divorce his wife).*

Polygamy is also practiced by some but this again opposes the Word of God as God only made one Eve and not several for Adam. When Our Lord talks of marriage He talks in the singular not in the plural. Martin Luther, the German reformer, however, allowed the double marriage of Landgraf Philip of Hessen who had the reputation of being 'The most immoral of princelings.' Philip married Christiana, daughter of the Duke of Saxony before he was twenty and she was eighteen. He admits that he could not remain faithful to his wife. He was attracted to Margaret von der Saal, a seventeen year old lady-in-waiting. So he sought Luther's advice about a double wedding. Luther and Melancthon stated (10th December 1539) that a general law that a man may have more than one wife could not be handed down but that a dispensation could be granted and that all knowledge of the dispensation and the marriage should be hidden from the public. 'All gossip on the subject is to be ignored as long as we are right in conscience, and we hold this is right.' 'What is permitted in Mosaic law is not forbidden in the Gospel' (De Wette-Seidemann, VI, 239-244; "Corp. Ref," III, 856-863).

The marriage took place on 4th March 1540. Later when the marriage became public knowledge Luther tried to deny it with a lie (Cambridge Hist. 11, 241). 'The secret 'yea' must for the sake of the Christian church remain a public 'nay.'" (De Witte-Seidemann, Op. Cit. VI, 263) 'What harm would there be, if a man, to accomplish better things and for the sake of the Christian church, does tell a good thumping lie.' (Lenz, "Briefwechsel" 382; Kolde, "Analecta," 356). This was his explanation and plea before the Hessia Counsellors assembled at Eisenach (1540). But polygamy is against the will of God and no reason, no justification, can change God's will and anyone who opposes the will of Christ and His Church only weakens the Christian Church, not strengthens it.

It is important that not only Christians but all people come to understand the importance of marriage. Marriages are the building blocks of society. So if marriages are strong and full of love; love of each other in the love of God, then society will be strong and loving. As people live in loving marriages, compassion, understanding, caring and sacrificing for others becomes part of life. This then is reflected in society and society then becomes more like it was supposed to be; a union of loving people one in their love of God and each other. Marriage also, when it is lived in the right way, is a blessing for the children that God may give to the husband and wife. As in a good marriage children grow up knowing they are loved and they are cared for. Children also grow knowing how to love and care for others and so when they enter society as adults the influence they may bring is a good one and so the strengthening of society continues.

The wonderful gift of marriage is not only for those personally involved but it is for all of society, for all the world so that it may grow in love, love of each other and love of God.

Homosexuality

Homosexuality has already had some discussion in the chapters on the 'priesthood' and 'marriage,' but it is important to look a little more closely at it, because many people see nothing wrong with homosexuality and see it as an acceptable choice or a right.

Anyone living the Christian faith should not accept homosexuality as right or natural, not even if the whole world accepts this. It is clear in the Holy Word of God in Holy Scripture, that God created man and woman *(Gn 1:27 Male and female he created them)* to be united in love so that, amongst other reasons, children could come into the world *(Gn 1:28 Be fertile and multiply).* If homosexuality were a natural relationship that all can live to if they so desire, eventually mankind as a species would cease to exist as there would be no or not enough children for the species to continue.

The partner God made for man was the flesh of his flesh *(Gn 2:23 This one, at last, is bone of my bones and flesh of my flesh; this one shall be called woman)* Eve, a woman, so from the beginning of mankind God set in place the relationship, the union of love that He wanted.

In the world today there are those who try to change this and sometimes use the excuse that homosexuality has been around for thousands of years so it cannot be wrong. It is true that throughout the history of mankind there have been homosexuals but this way of living came because of man's original sin which deteriorated mankind's morals so as to accept almost anything. God reminded the world of this when He destroyed Sodom and Gomorrah *(Gn 18 and19).* This excuse also is not valid because people could then say the same about any sin. Murder, stealing, lying, all would become acceptable because of their historical background. It is also claimed it is a right to be a homosexual, a right that is even taught in some schools! In Holy Scripture it is clear homosexuality is not right but wrong *(Lev 18:22 You shall not lie with a male as with a woman; such a thing is an abomination. Lev 20:13 If a man lies with a male as with a woman, both of them shall be put to death for their abominable deed. Rom 1:26-27 Their females exchanged natural relations for unnatural and the males likewise gave up natural relations with females and burned with lust for one another. Males did shameful things with males. 1 Corin 6:9 Active homosexuals will not inherit the kingdom of heaven. 1 Tim 1:9-10 The godless and sinful, the unholy and profane-practicing homosexuals).*

Homosexuality directly opposes the will of God and degrades the true love that is meant to be between people. It is extremely important to remember that no one should condemn another if the other is a homosexual. No person has the right to condemn another, only God has that right. It should also be remembered not to discriminate against homosexuals, that they too deserve to be treated with love, compassion and respect. It is the duty of every Christian to reach out to those with this disorder offering them help to come to terms with their unnatural desires so that a person who is homosexual can find a way to control their desires. If a Christian is homosexual it is essential they do not live a homosexual life but abstain from such a practice.

All those who love God and wish to follow God's way, Christ's way, should be praying for those afflicted with homosexuality to be cured of their disorder. As well as this all Christians should be standing up and proclaiming to their governments and to the world that homosexuality is not acceptable as a legal and binding relationship within society, that homosexuality should not be part of educational instructions on sex in schools. Also that homosexuality should not be paraded before the public in entertainment because this lowers the resistance in society to what is wrong and what is immoral, especially in the young people who can be so easily influenced by movie, television and music stars. This proclamation of God's truth must always though be done in love, in truth, in gentleness and in compassion but done with a firm grip onto God's will for mankind in its truly loving relationships.

<u>Contraception</u>

Within all Christian denominations there are those who agree with the use of contraception. The excuses for this vary. Such as those who are not ready for children, those who do not want children, as it will cause them to change their lifestyle, or claim it is too expensive to raise children. Others see the population of the world as being too great with not enough resources to sustain such numbers. Some use it as a right to decide themselves when or not to have children. One of the arguments used to support contraception in the beginning was that if contraception were available to all it would reduce the number of abortions. This was another deception because now there are more abortions than before. Most of the excuses for using contraception either centre on self or come from a lack of understanding of the true facts or of God's will. It is for Christians essential if they want to live their faith, to first look and see what is God's will in this matter.

God, in His divine love and wisdom, created mankind's bodies to work in a certain way. That is His will. To alter or block the natural functions of a body opposes God's will, God's design, God's plan. God created mankind's bodies to procreate and to bring children into the world, even commanding mankind to do so *(Gn 1:28 God blessed them, saying 'Be fertile and multiply.' Gn 9:1 God blessed Noah and his sons and said to them, 'Be fertile and multiply.' Gn 35:11 'I am God almighty; be fruitful and multiply')*. In His blessing God also showed it was a sacred desire of His that mankind should have children *(Mal 2:15 And what does that one require but godly offspring)*. God also reminded mankind that children are a blessed gift from Him *(Ps 127:3 Children too are a gift from the Lord, the fruit of the womb, a reward. Ps 127:5 Blessed is a full quiver. 1 Chr 25:5 God gave Heman fourteen sons and three daughters. 1 Chr 26:5 For God blessed him. Deut 7:13 He will love and bless and multiply you. He will bless the fruit of your womb).*

So to interfere with or to alter the natural functions of a body with the intention of denying God's blessing is a rejection of God's will and a placing of man's will before the divine will. It is also a denial of God's blessing, not only for the people involved in doing so, but a denial of God's blessing for all of mankind. As the children who would have come into the world would have been an essential part of the family of mankind, no matter how small or how great their role may have been. St Paul reminds people of the importance of child bearing *(1 Tim 2:15 But she will be saved through motherhood, provided women persevere in faith and love and holiness, with self-control. 1 Tim 5:14 So I would like younger widows to marry have children).*

It should be obvious to all that if a body's natural function is altered it then becomes unnatural and now the body is not at ease in itself or in its existence and is open to disease. The various reports on the oral contraceptive suggesting an increase in risk of cancer, blood clots and infertility seem to confirm this. What happens also with contraception is that it often lowers people's respect for their bodies, bodies which are sacred gifts from God *(1 Corin 6:19 Do you not know your body is a temple of the holy Spirit within you, whom you have from God).*

With this lowering of respect many slip into multiple sexual relationships, which in turn become excuses to continue using contraception. A sinful circle. With multiple sexual relationships people lose sight of true love and then may find it hard to have a truly loving and committed relationship with one person in marriage as they are supposed to have. Today in society this is clearly seen by the amount of divorces, of broken families and broken people. Immorality abounds as people turn to multiple sexual partners. In this immorality and seeking of bodily pleasure sometimes people look for more to stimulate them and in so doing may slip into homosexuality and other unnatural sexual relationships and activities. Contraception is a great destroyer of society not only by the lives it stops coming to earth but by the lives it leads into immorality and loveless lives.

Many people saw the introduction of the oral contraceptive as a new freedom for women but what freedom has it brought? Women now are so often expected, even in their early teenage years, to have sexual relationships. It is seen by many as unusual not to have these relationships. Some have lost their modesty, which is a beautiful part of the female persona, whereby, women now actively and aggressively pursue many sexual relationships. As this has happened there are young women who feel they must do as others do to avoid being seen as weird or different. So are forced to behave in a way they really do not want to or feel pressured into having sex *(The Mirror U.K. 31/12/03 Two out of five young women have been pressured into having sex)*. So in some ways contraception makes women sexual slaves and not free at all. This is also true for men who now may be expected to have had several sexual partners in order to gain experience. Men are now expected to live up to a certain sexual standard, or they may be discarded. Men and women are both sometimes seen as objects of desire to satisfy sexual needs. So with contraception, whether physical or chemical, has come a change for the worse in the relationships between people and has truly enslaved so many.

What has come as well with this slavery is an increase in disease. A report in the U.K. 'Daily Telegraph' (10th December 2003) from the 'British Medical Association' states, 'One in ten teenage girls aged 16 to 19 had the sexually transmitted disease chlamydia, which can make women infertile and that the provision of sexual health services was 'woefully inadequate' for young people-access to service is key. Do we really expect a 15 year old schoolboy with gonorrhea to take time off school to visit his GP and talk about his sex life?' The report also stated, '...the next generation will be the most infertile and obese in the history of mankind.'

Obviously then sexually transmitted diseases have increased dramatically not only in the young but also in adults with of course the most well known being HIV/AIDS. So many people have become slaves to the diseases that are associated with the 'Free Love,' which reared its ugly head with the introduction of the oral contraceptive *(Gal 6:8 Because the one who sows for his flesh will reap corruption from the flesh)* and which truly demands a high payment.

There are people who want to plan when they should have children within their marriage. It is of course not wrong to do this. When it becomes wrong is when contraception is used for this planning. There are available to all, natural family planning methods, (i.e. The Billings Method) which work with the body's natural cycles so as to plan when to conceive or not to conceive. These are very effective, some with a 97% success rate. Interestingly, in China, a study involving 992 women cohabiting with proven fertility and aged between 24 and 35, (the women had all tried artificial means of contraception in the past) found the women were so content with the NFP that when the trial ended 98% of them continued using NFP. The pregnancy rate of those using NFP was 0.5%- representing a success rate of 99.5%. The pregnancies that did occur were due to human error. In those who used the NFP method correctly the pregnancy rate was 0% (Nanjing Municipal Family Planning Commission).

Natural family planning does not offend God and does not offend the human body. Today with so many looking to healthy diets, to natural or organic foods so as to avoid the chemicals in some processed foods, it seems strange so many are ready to take a chemical to alter bodily functions rather than adopt a natural way. Natural family planning is also a commitment of love between husband and wife where both work together in love of God and each other.

The over population and lack of resources argument is hard to sustain if people understand the whole world's population could fit easily into the USA. There is no lack of resources, just a misuse and misappropriation of them. For example, if all the money spent in wealthy countries to care for their gardens alone were spent on the poor there would be no poor. The money spent on arms would house, clothe and feed all of the poor. The money spent on the two wars with Iraq would feed the poor. The money spent on entertainment by the West would eliminate poverty. Then there are the food mountains in various countries, the destruction of food by some countries, i.e. in the USA if fruits do not appear attractive, if potatoes do not have a certain acidity they may be destroyed. In France farmers destroy tomatoes. In Australia tens of thousands of sheep were destroyed because the price of sheep dropped and it was not worth taking them to market. All this while people starve!! And of course the waste and corruption in various governments should not be forgotten either.

God has given mankind all it needs in this world. The sad thing is that mankind does not use much of what it is given correctly and does not share as it should. Mankind allows greed and selfishness to rule and then in blindness says there is not enough for all. Contraception and the excuses for using it...a blight upon the earth.

In Vitro-fertilization

Impaired fertility in men and women is roughly equal and for some people is caused by what is ingested, i.e. lead, pesticides, monosodium glutamate (MSG), coffee, antidepressants, tranquilizers, narcotics. The way people live and what they do can also affect fertility. Sexual activity can cause infertility as sexually transmitted diseases are the leading cause of infertility. The more partners a man or a woman has sexually the greater the risk of sexual transmitted diseases and for women pelvic inflammatory disease which can also lead to infertility. Multiple partners may also cause a woman to develop antibodies to sperm.

Smoking and alcohol can both cause lower sperm counts in men and women who smoke seem to take longer to conceive than non-smokers. Marijuana used at moderate levels, was found to stop ovulation in monkeys and that THC, found in marijuana, may be directly toxic to a developing egg (Dr Carol Grace Smith, 'Science', March 25th 1983). Abortion and hormonal methods of contraception and IUD's can cause infertility. It is interesting that in these times so many sweet innocents are aborted and yet there are so many people seeking to conceive through IVF. The world is killing babies while at the same time trying to make babies. What madness!

It seems mankind, in it's way of life, creates the problem and then tries to fix it and in turn creates yet more problems. It is God's desire and design that children are conceived from a human loving union in marriage. When this is not possible legitimate medical advice and help should be sought, but when these avenues have been exhausted people should then not turn to what, in God's eyes, is wrong.

Sometimes people have to accept God's will and unite with Him in their suffering. It is a great blessing to have children but it is not a right, it is not something people can demand. Children are a gift from God and not property created by people or science to order. As can be seen already the path of designer babies is being walked by some, as they decide whether to have a boy or girl. Soon maybe colour of eyes and hair, height intelligence, strength etc. Mankind has no right to do this and should not believe it has. Then there are the unused fertilized eggs that are discarded or destroyed or even experimented on. So many babies killed and all so some people's desire can be met. Sometimes it has to be accepted that we cannot always have what we want!

Of course it is sad when a married couple cannot have children, a terrible pain, a true hurt for some. Maybe though God is calling these couples into a special sacrificial service of love where they can adopt and look after unwanted children. The sweet little angels who need a family's love and who can give their love to a family.

Mary

The role of Mary, the Mother of God, is disputed by many Christians. Some Christians have a strong love of Mary, others have no interest in Mary at all and there are some who reject Mary with almost a hatred for her.

Mary is the Mother of God, is the mother of Jesus as confirmed in Holy Scripture *(Luke 1:43 The mother of my Lord. Luke 1:35 The child to be born will be called holy, the Son of God. Mt 1:23 They shall name him Emmanuel, which means 'God is with us.' Gal 4:4 God sent his Son, born of a woman)*. This fact in itself should bring all Christians, all brothers and sisters of Christ, all imitators of Christ, to call Mary mother and to respect her *(Mt 2:11 Mary his mother)*. For if God loved Mary so much as to make her the mother of His Son, all who loved God should love Mary too otherwise it is a denial of God's love in His divine choice of Mary, His favour to Mary *(Luke 1:30 You have found favour with God)*.

It must offend Jesus Our Lord if people reject, dislike or say unkind things about His Mother Mary, just as it would offend most people if their mothers were treated so. It is through Our Lord Jesus people became children of God. Through Him we received adoption, it is also true that through Him and in Him, people also became adopted children of Mary *(Gal 4:4-6 God sent his Son, born of woman, born under the law, to ransom those under the law so that we might receive adoption. As proof that you are children, God sent the Spirit of his Son into our hearts).* The Spirit of the Lord told Mary she was to be the mother of God *(Luke 1:31 You will conceive in your womb and bear a Son and you shall name him Jesus. He will be great and called Son of the Most High).* So when the Spirit of God comes into peoples' hearts the Holy Spirit calls out the Word of God, that Mary is the Mother of God, whom all should favour and all should accept as their mother *(Jn 19:27 Behold your mother)* through adoption in Jesus the Lord, her Son.

God sent His Son to earth through a Blessed woman, in fact the most Blessed of women *(Luke 1:42 Most blessed are you among women).* God, who is pure love, where no sin resides *(1 Jn 3:3 As he is pure. Heb 4:15 Without sin)* or can reside, would then have to come to earth through a vessel that was pure, otherwise through the stain of sin on that vessel, God too would be stained with sin and that is impossible. So God in His mercy created Mary pure, created her Blessed and full of grace. It is in the same passage that not only is Mary declared Blessed but also the fruit of her womb *(Luke 1:42 And blessed is the fruit of your womb).* The fruit of her womb, pure from the pure vessel, Blessed from the Blessed vessel. It should also be noted that in the Word of God all generations are called to declare Mary 'Blessed' *(Luke 1:48 From now on will all ages call me blessed).*

The virginity of Mary is also a cause of disagreement.

The Latin and Eastern Rites agree that Mary was a virgin before, during and after the birth of Our Lord Jesus. However, some of the newer denominations disagree with this. Once again, looking to Holy Scripture the answer can be found *(Luke 1:27 To a virgin, betrothed to a man named Joseph, of the House of David, and the virgin's name was Mary. Luke 1:34 How can this be, since I have no relations with a man? Mt 1:22-23 All this took place to fulfil what the Lord had said through the prophet: 'Behold, the virgin shall be with child and bear a son, and they shall name him Emmanuel').* The child Jesus was conceived not by human seed or human means but by the power of the Holy Spirit *(Luke 1:35 The holy Spirit will come upon you and the power of the Most High will overshadow you. Mt 1:20 For it is through the holy Spirit that this child has been conceived in her).*

Interestingly, in the early years of the Church there was a strong opposition to this by non believers, Jews and pagans: *(St Justin, Dial. 99, 7: Pg 6, 708-709. Origen, Contra Celsum 1.32, 69: Pg 11, 720-721).* Yet the Church held firmly to this belief when it would have been so easy to deny it. By the Word of God, as declared in Holy Scripture, Mary was a virgin before and during the conception of the Lord Jesus. She also remained this way throughout her pregnancy *(Mt 1:25 He had no relations with her until she bore a Son and he named him Jesus).* It is also from this passage some believe that Joseph then began to have relations with Mary and that she bore him several children. If Mary did not have other children how would it be possible to know that Joseph had sexual relations with her? There is a belief this is confirmed by the mention of his family *(Mt 13:55-56 Is he not the carpenter's son? Is not his mother named Mary and his brothers James, Joseph, Simon and Judas? Are not his sisters all with us? Mk 6:3 Is he not the carpenter, the son of Mary and the brother of James and Joses and Judas and Simon? And are not his sisters all with us?).* But in those times not only immediate family were called brothers and sisters, so were cousins and did not even the apostles and disciples call each other brothers *(Acts 1:15 Peter stood up in the midst of the brothers. Acts 1:16 He said, 'My brothers...' Acts 7:2 And he replied, 'My brothers and fathers listen.' Acts 15:7 Peter got up and said to them, 'My brothers.' Acts 15:13 James responded, 'My brothers.' Acts 21:40-Acts 22:1 Paul stood on the steps and motioned with his hands to the people; and when all was quiet he addressed them in Hebrew, 'My brothers and fathers.' Acts 23:1 Paul looked intently at the Sanhedrin and said, 'My brothers.' 1 Corin 1:10 'I urge you brothers')*.

There are numerous times this terminology was used, these are but a few to show how the words 'fathers,' 'brothers' and 'sisters' were seen and used in society at the time. In Matthew and John it was seen that the Mary who was the mother of James and Joseph was in fact the sister of Mary, Jesus' Mother *(Mt 27:55-56 There were many women there, looking on from a distance who had followed Jesus from Galilee, ministering to him. Among them was Mary Magdalene and Mary the mother of James and Joseph. Jn 19:25 Standing by the cross were his mother and his mother's sister, Mary the wife of Clophas and Mary of Magdala)*. Jesus is also mentioned as 'The Son of Mary,' *(Mk 6:3 the son of Mary)* this is a singular term not plural, as would be with 'A Son of Mary.' As Our Lord was dying on the cross He asked John to take care of His Mother *(Jn 19:26-27 When Jesus saw his mother and the disciple there whom he loved, he said to his mother, 'Woman, behold your son.' Then he said to the disciple, 'Behold your mother' and from that moment the disciple took her into his home.)* Surely if the Lord Jesus had brothers and sisters He would have asked them to take care of Mary as tradition expects them to. If Mary had other children wouldn't they be there to look after her, especially the next eldest son, as was normal in those times?

It is believed by some that those who pray before statues and paintings of the Blessed Mother Mary or pray the Rosary are praying to Mary and not to God. This is a misunderstanding of what is taking place. When people pray in these ways what they are doing is joining together with their mother in heaven to pray to God. Our Lady unites in prayer with the people to worship, honour and adore God. Who better to join in prayer with than she whom is called 'Blessed' by an Archangel or she whom we are told has found favour with God? Who better to pray with than Our Lord's Mother?

When people pray the Rosary they are saying the 'Our Father,' the prayer the Lord asked people to pray in Holy Scripture. In the 'Hail Mary's' that are recited, again the words the Archangel said to Mary in Holy Scripture are being said, plus an asking of Mary to 'pray for us sinners.' The 'Glory Be' is a prayer glorifying God the Father and the Son and Holy Spirit with its roots in Holy Scripture.

The focus of the Rosary is from Holy Scripture; How Our Lady conceived. When she visited Elizabeth. The birth of Our Lord. His presentation. His finding in the temple. The agony in the garden. The scourging. The crowning of thorns. The carrying of the cross. The crucifixion. The resurrection. The ascension. The descent of the Holy Spirit. The assumption of Our Lady. The crowning as Queen of Heaven. The Baptism in the Jordan. The wedding feast of Cana. The declaration and proclaiming of the Kingdom of God. The Transfiguration. The Last Supper. So when people pray the Rosary they are reciting Holy Scripture and focusing on Holy Scripture united in prayer to God with the Mother of God, Mary most Holy. What can be wrong with that?

Repetitious Prayer

It is argued that this is repetitious prayer and that Holy Scripture says not to pray in this way *(Mt 6:7 In praying, do not babble like the pagans, who think that they will be heard because of their many words)*. Well, of course it is not babbling but a recital of Holy Scriptural words, Holy words. Our Lord Jesus Himself in Holy Scripture prayed repeatedly *(Mt 26:44 He left them and withdrew again and he prayed a third time saying the same thing again)*. St Paul tells us to *(1 Thess 5:17 'pray without ceasing')* and that he and others pray unceasingly *(1 Thess 1:2-3 We give thanks to God always for all of you, remembering you in our prayers unceasingly, calling to mind your work)*.

Even in heaven we are told of unceasing and repetitive prayer *(Rev 4:8 Day and night they do not stop exclaiming 'Holy, holy, holy is the Lord God almighty, who was and who is, and who is to come!')*. Praying to God over and over is not wrong, just as Our Lord explained when He taught on prayer *(Luke 11:5-8...Further teaching on prayer; He will get up to give him whatever he needs because of his persistence)*. It is when prayer is made other than to God, to evil and to false gods, it is wrong. All prayer of love, in love and for love to God is beautiful and the more that it is said the more that beauty is seen by God and by man.

Statues

Some claim by praying before a statue people are worshipping idols *(Ex 20:4 You shall not carve idols for yourselves)*. With a full reading of this chapter in Holy Scripture it shows that this was in reference to the idols made of the many Gods of those days *(Ex 20:3-5 You shall not have other gods beside me. You shall not carve idols for yourselves in the shape of anything in the sky above or the earth below or in the waters beneath the earth. You shall not bow down before them or worship them)*. If this were not so, why then would Moses later ask for Cherubim? For surely they would be idols and Moses would be breaking the Word of God! *(Ex 25:18 Make two cherubim of beaten gold)*. Or why would God ask Moses to make a serpent thereby breaking His own Word *(Num 21:8-9 And the Lord said to Moses, 'Make a saraph and mount it on a pole, and if anyone who has been bitten looks at it, he will recover. Moses, accordingly made a bronze serpent and mounted it upon a pole)*.

God also called people to look at this holy statue so as to be healed, so it seems God, through this image made by Moses, poured out healing grace. King Solomon, when he built the temple, also had statues of Cherubim and other images in the temple *(1 Kings 6:23-29, 1 Kings 7:25-44)*.

From Holy Scripture, it can be seen that when the statues or images made are those that glorify God, *(2 Thess 1:10 To be glorified among his holy ones)* lead people to God, to holiness, or remind people of God's power and love in lives, as can be seen in the statues and images of saints, there is nothing wrong with this. On the contrary, doing this can bring people closer to God, as God, through that image, may, as He did with the serpent, pour out His healing grace to touch peoples' lives to heal and convert them.

<u>Venerating Saints</u>

It is not worshipping false idols when people pray in front of statues of Our Lady or saints. These statues remind people of the total commitment these holy men and women have made to God and are examples for people to follow in their lives so that they too can live as the holy ones did. *(Heb 13:7 Remember your leaders who spoke the word of God to you. Consider the outcome of their way of life and imitate their faith).*

In the various saints' lives, it can be seen how God worked through their weaknesses to bring them to holiness. Reflecting on this and as people think of the saints, it reminds them that no matter how weak a person is or how much they may have fallen, God is there waiting to bring each one to holiness as He did with the saints. It also can be seen how God gave each saint the strength in His love, to persevere and to overcome all opposition. Reminding all people this strength can be theirs as well if they try to live holy lives just as the saints did. *(2 Thess 2:16-17 May our Lord Jesus Christ himself and God our Father, who has loved us and given us everlasting encouragement and good hope through his grace, encourage your hearts and strengthen them in every good deed and word.)* Live lives of love, of service, of obedience in and to God's Holy will.

Praying to the Saints

As death does not separate a person from Our Lord *(Rom 8:38 For I am convinced that neither death... Rom 8:39 will be able to separate us from the love of God in Christ Jesus our Lord)* and Christians are all one in Him, *(Eph 4:4 One body and one Spirit, as you were also called to one hope. Col 3:15 In one body)* then those who have died in Him remain one with those living on earth in Him, remain one in His body *(Eph 1:22-23 The church, which is his body)* and remain one with those in His Church.

There is then three levels of the Church the body of Christ: Those on earth, those in purgatory and those in heaven. A Trinitarian Church which is one in God. Just as it is a normal part of faith to ask someone in the Church on earth to pray for an intention or to join in prayer *(Rom 15:30 Join me in the struggle by your prayers to God on my behalf. 2 Thess 1:11 We always pray for you. 2 Thess 3:1 Pray for us)* so too it should be a normal part of faith to ask the saints in heaven who are part of the Church to pray for and with people. The saints, whom it is known from Holy Scripture, pray in heaven *(Rev 5:8 The prayers of the holy ones. Rev 5:11 The voices of many angels and the living creatures and the elders. They were countless in number and they cried out in a loud voice, 'Worthy is the lamb that was slain...' Rev 6:9-10 I saw underneath the altar the souls of those who had been slaughtered because of the witness they bore to the word of God. They cried out in a loud voice...)* and who love to join in with those on earth in prayer as witnesses to their faith *(Heb 12:1 We are surrounded by so great a cloud of witnesses)*.

Some still believe it is wrong to pray with the dead but it is to be remembered that those who die in Christ Our Lord come to eternal life in Him and so are alive with Him and in Him *(1 Corin 15:22 For just as in Adam all die, so too in Christ all shall be brought to life.*

Mk 12:27 He is not God of the dead but of the living. Jn 6:58 Unlike your ancestors who ate and still died, whoever eats this bread will live forever). The Church of Our Lord is His living body on earth, in purgatory and in heaven.

Purgatory

The existence of purgatory is denied or doubted by some, yet there are various references to it in the Word of God. Purgatory is where people go to be purified so that they can enter heaven. In heaven no sin resides and so nothing with sin on it can enter heaven *(Rev 21:27 Nothing unclean will enter it)*. That in turn means that those who sin and die cannot enter heaven without that sin being cleansed and atoned for and, of course, we all sin *(1 Jn 1:8 If we say, 'We are without sin, we deceive ourselves and the truth is not in us.' James 3:2 For we all fall short in many respects)*.

Some wonder, if sins have been confessed, why then would they go to purgatory. Firstly, does everyone confess truly all their sins and atone for them? There are those who hold onto sin, hiding their wrongs away. Then there are those who confess but do not atone for the wrongs they may have done and do not change the way they live so as to avoid sin. In the Old Testament even David had to atone after being forgiven *(2 Sam 12:13-14 Then David said to Nathan, 'I have sinned against the Lord.' Nathan answered David, 'The Lord on his part has forgiven your sin; you shall not die. But since you have utterly spurned the Lord by this deed the child born to you must surely die.')*.

There are those who believe if they follow certain devotions they will go straight to heaven, but this is only true if they also live the way God calls them to. To truly follow a devotion is not to only say the prayers, keep the images or wear the signs, it is also to live the faith! To believe that a person can live a life of doing wrong but that by following a special devotion they will go straight to heaven, avoiding purgatory is certainly a misunderstanding of faith. To live the faith is to strive for holiness at all times and in all things, not just in a few *(Heb 12:14 Strive for peace with everyone and for that holiness without which no one will see the Lord)*.

Our Lord referred to purgatory and paying for sins committed *(Mt 5:26 Amen, I say to you, you will not be released until you have paid the last penny).* St Peter also talked about the prison our Lord meant *(1 Peter 3:19-20 He also went to the spirits in prison who had once been disobedient)* and there is confirmation that people will be called to account for their sins after death *(Mt 12:32 Whoever speaks against the holy Spirit will not be forgiven, either in this age or the age to come).* So there must be an age to come where after death sins can be forgiven *(Mt 12:36 I tell you on the day of judgement people will render an account for every careless word they speak. 1 Peter 4:5-6 They will give an account to him who stands ready to judge the living and the dead. For this is why the gospel was preached even to the dead that, though condemned in the flesh, in human estimation they might live in the spirit in the estimation of God).* It becomes clear from Holy Scripture that sins can be atoned for after death, *(2 Macc 12:46 Thus he made atonement for the dead that they might be freed from this sin)* and that the living can be part of this atonement *(1 Corin 15:29 Otherwise what will people accomplish having themselves baptized for the dead?).*

It is in purgatory that people are brought to perfection by the cleansing love and mercy of God. The cleansing fire of the Spirit *(1 Corin 3:15 The person will be saved but only as through fire).* So that they can then reside with the perfect One in His eternal home.

No one should be afraid of purgatory for it is through purgatory so many enter into the glory of God in heaven. Purgatory, a holy place where people are brought to complete holiness.

Speaking to the Dead

Clairvoyants, those who claim to speak to the dead, are often sought for advice and help by Christians. Performances of those who claim they can speak to the dead are well attended or watched by many Christians. Yet this goes against the Holy Scripture and Church teachings *(Deut 18:10-12 Nor a fortune teller, soothsayer, charmer, diviner, or caster of spells, nor one who consults ghosts and spirits or seeks oracles from the dead. Anyone who does such things is an abomination to the Lord. Acts 16:16-19 St Paul casts out oracular spirit).* It is very dangerous for Christians or for anyone to pay attention to these people, as it is evil spirits that speak to them, *(1 Jn 4:6 The spirit of deceit)* not the dead. After death there are only three realities and they are heaven, purgatory and hell. Anything else is a deception from evil.

Those who believe in clairvoyants because they may have been told some truths about their lives that only they could know, should understand that Satan and the other evil ones know everything about people's lives. The evil ones use this knowledge to deceive people trying to turn them from God. The evil ones will even, if necessary, say good things so as to confuse and lead away from God and to weaken peoples' faith. The evil ones will even declare that Jesus is the Son of God if it suits their purpose *(Mt 8:29 They cried out, 'What have you to do with us Son of God?' James 2:19 You believe that God is one. You do well. Even the demons believe that and tremble).* Generally, however, most of what they say is just a recounting of past events or past relationships and God does not get mentioned and most of what they say is trivial *(1 Tim 4:1 Now the spirit explicitly says that in the last times some will turn away from the faith by paying attention to deceitful spirits and demonic instructions).*

God sometimes in His mercy allows saints and angels from Heaven to appear and speak to people. Helping, encouraging and guiding to holy lives. Those in purgatory may very briefly appear in people's minds so as to remind their friends or relatives to pray for them. All else comes from Hell, comes from evil and comes to deceive, hurt and to destroy faith. It is also important not to believe because a 'psychic' or 'clairvoyant' prays before a sitting that what they receive is good, is from God. It is not uncommon for those who pray to still be deceived by evil, to be confused and to be led astray. Anyone involved in these ways is involved in evil ways and not in Christ, Our Lord's ways and all Christians should avoid these spiritual deceptions.

Faith

It is taught by some churches that Christians are justified by 'faith alone' and not by the works people do *(Martin Luther, 'Treatise of Good Works' 1520).* Yet nowhere in Holy Scripture does it say this! However, in the Bible, the Apostle James does say that works are an essential part of faith and that yes, people are justified by works! *(James 2:18-22 Indeed some might say, 'You have faith and I have works,' demonstrate your faith to me without works and I will demonstrate my faith to you from my works. You believe that God is one. You do well. Even the demons believe that and tremble. Do you want proof, you ignoramus, that faith without works is useless? Was not Abraham our father justified by works when he offered his son Isaac upon the altar? You see that faith was active along with his works and faith was completed by the works. James 2:24 See how a person is justified by works and not by faith alone. James 2:26 For just as a body without a spirit is dead, so also faith without works is dead).*

Even Our Lord sent the apostles and disciples out to work *(Mt 10:5 Jesus sent out these twelve. Mt 10:7-8 As you go make this proclamation, 'The kingdom of heaven is at hand.' Cure the sick, raise the dead, cleanse lepers, drive out demons. Mk 6:7 He summoned the twelve and began to send them out two by two and gave them authority over unclean spirits. Luke 10:1 After this the Lord appointed seventy two others whom he sent ahead of him in pairs. Luke 10:9 Cure the sick in it and say to them, 'The kingdom of God is at hand for you').* Surely then every Christian as a disciple is called to holy work *(Phil 2:13 For God is the one who, for his good purpose, works in you both to desire and to work)* as it is through the work of God that 'The Kingdom of God' can be seen in living faith. Again Our Lord reminds people *(Mt 25:34-46)* to work in love of Him in all they do and to see Him in every person they help with holy work, and that in this work righteousness can be found.

If the Lord had taught 'faith alone,' then after Pentecost the apostles would not have needed to go out and work in spreading His love. They could have gathered together in faith and prayed, leaving it all to God, having faith in Him doing all that was necessary to build the Church. However, they knew God called them to work for Him so that through their sacrifices and struggles the disciples could unite with Him in the carrying of the cross. Without the work of the early Church and the witness of these works, many may not even have heard of Our Lord and believed in Him.

Today the same is true, if people sit back and do little saying, 'My faith has saved me and I will leave everything to God,' they may then be denying others the opportunity to know Jesus. Every Christian *(Eph 2:10 Created in Christ Jesus for the good works)* is called to work for Our Lord and for their brothers and sisters, *(Acts 20:35 In every way I have shown you that by hard work of that sort we must help the weak and keep in mind the words of the Lord Jesus who himself said, 'It is more blessed to give than to receive.')* as it is in that work their love of God, their strength of faith and their righteousness can be seen and can grow. It is in that giving many will find blessedness *(Rom 2:7 Eternal life to those who seek glory, honour and immortality through perseverance in good works).*

Faith comes from love, the love of God for mankind and peoples' love of God. So faith is a gift of love from God to be lived in love. Those who accept the Lord Jesus' offer of salvation surely know that His sacrifice is the sacrifice of love and that it is through Him lovingly carrying mankind's sins on the cross people can find justification in Him. A justification that is given in love and to be accepted in love with faith in the Lord. God is love *(1 Jn 4:8 For God is love)* and so love must be the greatest gift. Without love, faith is dead *(1 Corin 13:2 If I have all faith so as to move mountains but do not have love, I am nothing).* So it is love that makes faith and works good, acceptable and worthy, not faith alone as stated by Martin Luther, 'A Treatise on Good Works' 'Faith alone makes all other works good, acceptable and worthy.' Faith then comes from God who is love and so must come from love. Faith is an expression of that love, as are works. It is in love faith exists and in love faith and works are woven together *(Gal 5:6 But only faith working through love. 1 Corin 13:13 So faith, hope and love remain, these three; but the greatest of these is love).*

It appears then the teaching of 'Sola Fide' or 'Faith Alone' is an addition to, *(as Luther had to insert the German word for 'alone' into Romans 3:28)* and misinterpretation of Holy Scripture *(Mk 7:7 In vain do they worship me, teaching as doctrines human precepts. Rev 22:18 I warn everyone who hears the prophetic words in this book: If anyone adds to them, God will add to him the plagues described in this book)* as it is nowhere to be found in the original Word of God. In fact the reverse is found. The Lord Jesus actually says, in Matthew 25:34-46, that through good works righteousness can be found.

<u>Tradition</u>

There is also a belief that it is from Holy Scripture all authority comes and that tradition has no authority within the Church *(Mt 15:3 Why do you break the commandments of God for the sake of tradition? Mk 7:8 You disregard God's commandment but cling to human tradition. Col 2:8 See to it that no one captivate you with an empty seductive philosophy according to human tradition according to the elemental powers and not according to Christ).*

Of course, if tradition is put in place of the Commandments or tradition is not according to the will of Christ Our Lord and what He passed on through the apostles, then it has no authority in the Church. If, though, the traditions followed are those passed from the Lord to the apostles and through them passed onto the Church, or if the tradition is taken from Holy Scripture, it cannot be wrong and bears the authority of Christ Our Lord and is sacred. *(1 Corin 11:2 And hold fast to the traditions just as I handed them onto you. 2 Thess 2:15 Therefore brothers, stand firm and hold fast to the traditions that you were taught, either by an oral statement or by a letter of ours).*

The apostles, who were companions of Our Lord as He walked the earth, learned a great amount from Him. *(2 Peter 1:16 We did not follow cleverly devised myths when we made known to you the power and coming of Our Lord Jesus Christ, but we have been eyewitnesses of his majesty. Eph 3:5 As it has now been revealed to his holy apostles and prophets by the Spirit)* So much in fact that not all was written down in Holy Scripture.*(Jn 21:25 There are also many other things that Jesus did, but if these were to be described individually, I do not think the whole world would contain the books that would be written).* It is through the words and traditions the apostles passed on in the Holy Apostolic Church that we get insight and instruction about some of these other things. Where better to get them from?

(Mt 23:3 Therefore, do and observe all things whatsoever they tell you).

St Paul confirms that he passed on by word of mouth the divine message and tradition of Our Lord Jesus, *(2 Tim 1:13-14 Take as your norm the sound words that you heard from me, in the faith and love that are in Christ Jesus. Guard this rich trust with the help of the holy Spirit. 1 Corin 15:3 For I handed onto you as of first importance what I also received)* and that the Church, the faithful, should use this to teach others *(2 Tim 2:2 And what you heard from me through many witnesses entrust to faithful people who will have the ability to teach others as well).* Because the faith for many will come from what they hear and what they are taught *(Rom 10:17 Thus faith comes from what is heard).*

Now it becomes clear that not only is Holy Scripture authoritative but so, too, is sacred tradition. That it is Holy Scripture and sacred tradition bound together that bring a fuller and truer understanding of the will of Christ Our Lord for His Church. This is why the Holy Apostolic Church does not change with the times but holds to the tradition passed on by the apostles.

Martin Luther, in 'An open letter to the Christian nobility of The German Nation' (1520), suggests that every person has the right to decide, 'The power to test and judge what is correct or incorrect in matters of faith.' 'What squares with faith and what does not' and to interpret Holy Scripture in their own way. 'According to our interpretation of the Scriptures.' In England William Tyndale, writer of 'The English Bible' also taught that every person can interpret the Bible in their own way.

St Peter reminds people that this is not so *(2 Peter 1:20 There is no prophecy of scripture that is a matter of personal interpretation)* and of the dangers when this happens *(2 Peter 3:15-17 Paul, according to the wisdom given to him, also wrote to you, speaking of these things as he does in all his letters. In them there are some things hard to understand that the ignorant and unstable distort to their own destruction, just as they do the other scriptures. Therefore beloved since you are forewarned, be on your guard not to be led into the error of the unprincipled).*

If a person is seriously ill they would not stop passers-by in the street, explain their illness to them, then ask the peoples' advice on how to treat the illness and follow it. Firstly, there would be many different answers, so which to follow? Secondly, for a serious illness most people would not know the correct answer. The best thing to do would be to go to a doctor who was trained to deal with the illness, a doctor who understood the illness and to get help from this doctor. Holy Scripture, which is so deep that it will never be fully understood until the glory of Heaven is reached, would be even more difficult for people to understand and to interpret.

It makes sense then that to come to a better understanding of Holy Scripture people should go to those who study it, who have the benefit of the knowledge of the great theologians and Doctors of the Church. To those who have the authority of the Lord and the wisdom of the Holy Spirit guiding them. Have the knowledge of the apostles passed on to them in word and in tradition, because it is here surely the clearest and most truthful teachings would come from, not from everyone's own individual opinion. It is here the best help could be found in finding the right way to walk the path of Jesus Our Lord.

Other Faiths

God loves all people and offers salvation to all through His Son and Our Lord Jesus *(1 Jn 2:2 And not for our sins only but for those of the whole world. Mt 28:19 Go therefore and make disciples of all nations. Mk 16:15 Go into the whole world and proclaim the gospel to every creature).* What about other faiths, will they be saved too? Ask some. God in His unfathomable divine mercy, which man cannot understand offers salvation to all people. Yes, even those who do not know His Son Jesus. If a person has never heard of the Lord, is that their fault? Or if a person has been taught by their society or their family to deny Jesus as the Son of God, but still to look for God in life. Are they to be condemned because of that? Of course not!

What God does is judge people on how they have tried to live to His will as they know it with a truthful heart and how they have sought God in their lives in the way they have known Him. His will is placed within all people and is an internal knowledge of good and bad, which is called a conscience. God in His love reaches out to these people of other faiths to embrace them and draw them into His heart and into His Heavenly Kingdom and many will find their way there *(Rev 15:4 All the nations will come and worship before you).*

However, if there are those who have not heard of Jesus the Lord, those who do not know Him, this also means maybe not all Christians have been working as missionaries for Christ in the world. It is the duty of all Christians to go and proclaim the good news of salvation so that all people on this planet can come to know and love Jesus in their lives. So that others can come to know the fullness of God and not just a part of Him.

Who will be judged worse? Someone who has not known the Lord Jesus but tried to live a good life and tried to live to God's way as they have known it? Or those who have known the fullness of God's love in Jesus but refused to share this knowledge with others, kept this knowledge to themselves and not behaved so well?

Just as the Jewish people were chosen for God to come to earth through, so that all could be saved, so too are Christians chosen to take the salvation of the Lord to all, so all can find the way to heaven in Him. In imitation of Christ Our Lord, who suffered and sacrificed on the cross as He brought salvation to mankind, so too, His Christian people must be prepared to suffer and sacrifice in bringing Jesus' love and offer of salvation to all. In a similar way to Our Lord calling impure beings, humans, into His pure love so that they could find perfection in Him, holiness in Him, the Church and all its members must call all people into the fullness of God's truth on earth. So that all people can find the faith that will lead them into the pure love of Christ and in Him and in His body find holiness. Not doing so may deny others the knowledge of Christ's love in life and many may deny themselves the opportunity of truly being Christ-like.

Tolerance between Faiths

While Christians cannot allow other faiths, other beliefs to change what Christ, Our Lord gave to mankind, Christians must be tolerant of other faiths. God in His Divine wisdom, gives every person the freedom to choose what they live to and what they believe *(2 Corin 3:17 And where the Spirit of the Lord is, there is freedom).* So too then must Christians as imitators of Jesus. As Christians, those in the Church must accept the rights of others to their belief systems, while gently and lovingly encouraging others to come to know the Divine love of Jesus, Our Lord.

This tolerance should also be shown to Christians by those of other faiths, for Christians also have the right to worship God freely.

Sadly, in the world this God-given freedom is frequently denied. Some faiths expect freedom for their followers but deny the same freedom to other faiths. Most Christian countries do allow this freedom of faith but some do not. What happened in the former Yugoslavia is an example of this where Christians killed Muslims, Muslims killed Christians and Christians even killed other Christians because of differences of faith. Also in some Muslim countries Christians are killed and churches are burned, while in some Christian countries Mosques are attacked. This is happening around the world and yet governments do so little at times to stop it. Some governments even support religious discrimination i.e. Saudi Arabia, where Christians may be imprisoned for praying together. Russia permits some faiths but denies others.

No government, no church and no people should discriminate against others because of faith and none should try to force their beliefs on others. As doing so denies the gift of freedom that is God-given.

Just as other faiths demand and expect religious freedom for their followers, all Christian governments and churches should insist and expect freedom of faith for Christians worldwide, for this is the right of all.

War

Today there seems to be a lot of uncertainty and confusion amongst Christians and especially Catholics as to war and whether or not to support peace or war. As Christians it is important that we place Christ Our Lord and His teachings above all else, even our human loyalties, just as the early Church did and just as the saints and martyrs did.

When Our Lord came to earth He proclaimed peace, love and forgiveness. Today, however, many people claim the times and situation to be different. How different are they? At the time of Our Lord the Romans occupied the Holy Land. Many were killed, tortured, enslaved or oppressed by the Romans or their puppets. The Zealots and others hoped the Messiah would come and free them from this and bring them to victory over their enemies.

However, Our Lord Jesus came and proclaimed peace, love and forgiveness, not force of arms. He taught this clearly *(Mt 5:39 'But I say to you offer no resistance to one who is evil. When someone strikes you on your right cheek turn the other one to him as well.' Mt 5:44 'Love your enemies.' Luke 6:27-29 'But to you who hear I say, love your enemies, do good to those who hate you, bless those who curse you, pray for those who mistreat you. To the person who strikes you on one cheek offer the other as well').*

These teachings, with the Commandment 'Thou shalt not kill,' appear to be some of the hardest for people to obey or follow. Often like the Pharisees, Sadducees and Scribes we make clever arguments to justify ignoring or changing our understanding of what God has said to mankind. Some claim that when Our Lord chased the money-changers from the temple using force He gave permission for us to use force against others. However, Our Lord did not kill these people even though with one word He could have done so.

Instead, He stopped the wrong they did, giving them then the opportunity in the rest of their lives to reflect on His actions and words.

Some quote the Catechism teaching on just war. There are those who look to the great Saints Thomas Aquinas and Augustine and use their words as justification for war. When Jesus Our Lord was confronted by the Jews over divorce they used the words of Moses to justify divorce. Yet Jesus replied, *(Mark 10:5 'Because of the hardness of your hearts he wrote you this commandment').*

Would Our Lord be saying this today to those who try to justify war by the words of St Thomas and St Augustine?

Some people believe that we must respond to evil with force of arms yet, Our Lord, by example, showed mankind another way to respond to evil. When He was abused, tortured, crucified and killed Our Lord only responded in love and forgiveness. Even though the Son of God had the power of heaven at His command and could have called on that power to destroy those who were treating Him so, He did not. Instead, He gave us the example which as Christians, as imitators of Christ, we are called to follow. *(Jn 13:15 I have given you a model to follow, so that as I have done for you, you should also do).*

Our Lord gave His life in love knowing it was this that would overcome evil *(Rom 12:17 Do not repay anyone evil for evil).* He showed us that we must be prepared to do the same in our lives if we are to be like Him and that we should not respond violently to violence *(1 Peter 2:21 For to this you have been called, because Christ also suffered for you, leaving you an example that you should follow in his footsteps).*

Our Lord also when He opened His arms on the cross in love opened a way for us to reach a deeper level of spirituality and higher levels of grace. In imitating

Christ Our Lord, by answering evil only with love and forgiveness, we can be lifted through the cross to a spiritual level of freedom which brings us to be grace-filled vessels of God's merciful love. This grace frees us from the chains of fear, as now in that grace we come to understand the power of God's sacrificial love. The power that nothing or no one can overcome. Filled with this power, the fear of death is taken from us and we come to see that this life is part of our eternal life in Christ Our Lord. That this life, though valuable, is only a moment in eternity. A moment to be lived for God so that the remainder of our eternal moments will be with Him in heaven.

With this realization comes the understanding that to cling to this life is futile and that while treasuring this life we should not be afraid to lose it for Christ Our Lord. Now without this chain shackling a person to the worldly life, the spiritual realm opens up as the scales fall from their spiritual sight. Now it becomes clear that even if it seems as if evil is victorious, it is not. Now one can see that even if the whole world is one day ruled by those who deny Christ this will only be short lived for the power of His victory will bring His glorious kingdom to earth regardless of the opposition to it. Now it becomes obvious God's victory does not depend on us, that instead we are called to be part of His victory by uniting with Him in His sacrificial love. Eyes are opened to see that if we imitate Our Lord by submitting to the all-powerful will of the Father unto death, we can be lifted on the cross with Christ Our Lord. Then through us His grace is poured out to touch and bless many others, bringing them to salvation in Him.

Today the fear of terrorism, the fear of our Muslim brothers and sisters ruling the world, the fear of evil, leads many to justify acts of war, to justify force of arms and to justify the taking of life in revenge. *(Mt 10:28 Do not be afraid of those who kill the body but cannot kill the soul. Rom 12 : 19 do not look for revenge).*

These fears trap many and many in fear deny themselves the opportunity that the saints and martyrs have embraced in the past, the opportunity of being lifted high in the grace of God. In denying themselves this grace they also deny others that would have been touched by that grace through them. In denying this grace, pain and suffering are allow to grow through the evil in the world that is not now confronted by the sacrificial love of the imitators of Christ *(Rom 12:21 Do not be conquered by evil but conquer evil with good).*

It is important for all Christians to consider what Christ calls them to and to answer that call in becoming sacrificial lambs of love prepared to give their all for Christ in spreading His love, His peace and His forgiveness. Just as He gave His life for us proclaiming love, peace and forgiveness to all, we too must proclaim peace to the world…not war *(Eph 2:17 He came and preached peace to you who were far off and peace to those who were near. Mt 5:9 Blessed are the peacemakers for they will be called the children of God).*

The Pope stated on January 12th 2004, to the Diplomatic Corps, 'We Christians have the responsibility to propound the Gospel of peace.'

Sanctity of Life

God has called mankind to respect, protect and treasure life, even giving the Commandment that people must not kill *(Ex 20:13 You shall not kill)*. Our Lord Jesus re-affirmed this in His Holy Word *(Mt 5:21-22 You have heard it was said to your ancestors, 'You shall not kill and whoever kills will be liable to judgement,' but I say to you whoever is angry with his brother is liable to judgement.' Mt 19:17-18 Keep the commandments. He asked him, 'Which ones?' and Jesus replied, 'Thou shalt not kill...' Mk 10:19 You know the commandments, 'You shall not kill...' Luke 18:20 'You shall not kill...')*. The instruction from God is very clear and for those who follow Christ Our Lord it is essential to follow what He says. Christians are called to put on the mind of Our Lord *(1 Corin 2:16 'But we have the mind of Christ')* and imitate Him in holding all life as precious and in rejecting the destroying of life.

There are Christians today who proclaim they are 'pro-life' because they rightly reject the terrible sin of abortion and stand firmly against it, as all are supposed to do. However, some of these same people support the death penalty or support wars of aggression. To be pro-life a person has to defend life from conception until natural death. Pro-lifers cannot be subjective for then they become pro-choice, choosing when to defend life and when not to. A pro-lifer cannot support life in one area and not in another. To be truly pro-life means to reject contraception, abortion, the death penalty, war of aggression and euthanasia. To reject anything that intentionally takes life.

The Pope has spoken very clearly against the taking of life. Yet some Christians, some Catholics, say that because he is the Pope, that is what he is meant to say. They then ignore the Holy Father's words when it suits them to. It seems some have forgotten that it is not only the Pope who is meant to speak this way but that all Christians are meant to speak this way too!

All life is precious, even that of the worst sinner and all life should be protected and defended by all Christians, for that is Christ's way.

End Times

Many predictions are made about the 'end times' and the second coming of Jesus. Some people who claim to know the 'end times' are coming encourage others to store food, water, money, even to build refuges where they can hide and be safe. Every disaster that happens and every unusual event is professed to be a sign of the 'end times.' Fear is entering the lives of many Christians as they wonder what lies ahead. People look at diseases like HIV/AIDS, SARS sweeping the world and say the 'end times' are coming, as if diseases have never taken a heavy toll on human life before. Yet, there was the Black Plague that decimated the populations of many countries. In the early 1900's the flu epidemic killed millions in Europe. Every time the terrible scourges of war or genocide break out, again people say the 'end times' are coming. Yet, there have been wars and genocide throughout mankind's history *(Mk 13:7 When you hear of wars and reports of wars do not be alarmed; such things must happen but it will not yet be the end).*

It seems many Christians have forgotten history and it also seems many have forgotten that the Lord told people in Holy Scripture that no one but the Father knows the 'end times' *(Mt 24:36 'But of that day and hour no one knows, neither the angels of heaven, nor the Son, but the Father alone. Mk 13:32 But of that day or hour no one knows, neither the angels in heaven, nor the Son, but only the Father. Mk 13:33 You do not know when the time will come).* So if anyone claims to know the 'end times,' they are denying the Word of God *(Luke 17:20-21 The coming of the kingdom of God cannot be observed and no one will announce 'Look here it is,' or, 'Look there it is').*

When Christians store food, water and goods because they fear the 'end times,' again this is an ignoring of the Lord in Holy Scripture *(Mt 6:25 Therefore I tell you, do not worry about your life, what you will eat or drink, or about your body. Luke 12:4 I tell you, do not be afraid of those who kill the body).* It also is not a living of their faith because now the people become self-centered. They worry about themselves, their family and maybe their friends. So in fear there is a blinding of what Christians should truly be doing.

In the Third World today, it is the 'end times' for many who starve, die from simple diseases and suffer in poverty. Christians in more affluent countries, instead of thinking of self and storing for what might happen in the future to them, should be giving to those in the Third World, those in need now and those living their 'end times' now. Evil has blinded many with fear and drawn them into self and away from sharing, caring and helping those in need. Drawn them away from the truly Christian life *(1 Jn 4:18 There is no fear in love, but perfect love drives out fear).*

The Holy Father, Pope John Paul II, as the year 2000 approached cautioned about making apocalyptic predictions. At a general assembly in St Peter's Square the Pope stated, 'Since Jesus said nothing about when the end would come, attempted predictions are baseless and misleading.' Again, on December 31st 2001 in his homily at an evening prayer service, the Pope said, 'It is a very human temptation to want to know what will happen in the future and in the end how much time is left. But when Jesus' disciples asked the same kind of questions Jesus told them that time was in hands of the Father.' He also stated, 'Jesus tells us not to uselessly question that which is reserved to God.' At a weekly audience in Feb. 2001,The Holy Father advised, 'The Kingdom of God will not have it's full establishment on earth through some apocalyptic event, but quietly and with the cooperation of men and women who work for justice and peace.'

Those who love Christ Our Lord and live to His way should know that their lives are in God's hands. That they will only die when God wants or allows it to happen and nothing or no one can change that. Knowing this, there should be no fear of the future, only security in God's love. There should be no fear of the 'end times' knowing when they come, for those who love Our Lord Jesus, they will lead to glory *(Luke 21:28 But when these signs begin to happen, stand erect and raise your heads, because your redemption is at hand).*

Antichrist

Many are afraid of an Antichrist coming and look for him everywhere. Once again, this is a blindness of faith because the Antichrist is everywhere: abortion, adultery, immorality, homosexuality, killing, wars, greed, selfishness, waste, hatred, racism, injustice, and all the other sins...these are Antichrist and when Christians accept these wrongs, they too become Antichrist *(1 Jn 2:22 Whoever denies the Father and the Son, this is the antichrist).* When Christians do not stand against these wrongs they allow the Antichrist in the world to grow *(Rom 14:22 Blessed is the one who does not condemn himself for what he approves).*

When the Antichrist will come in flesh no one but God knows but every Christian should know that if they hold firmly onto the love of Our Lord Jesus Christ, living the way He asks, then they have nothing to fear. Because no matter what happens, in Christ Our Lord people become victorious over evil, victorious over all that is Antichrist. Victorious over the Antichrist himself because their eternal being will be safe in the heart of Jesus. This is what Christians in faith are supposed to believe and in having that belief, that firm faith, there should be no fear, only certainty of victory, *(1 Jn 5:4 The victory that conquers the world is our faith).* Knowing that even if a Christian had to stand and face the Antichrist, their love of God and their strong faith would bring them the strength to defeat the Antichrist, because Christ Our Lord would give the person the holy power to do so *(Jn 1:5 And the darkness has not overcome it).*

The Christian faith is not one of fear, of defeat and uncertainty. The Christian faith is the faith of divine victorious love where no fear should reside, only the certainty of Our Lord Jesus' victory on the cross, in the resurrection and in every person who truly loves Him *(2 Corin 5:6 So we are always courageous).*

Signs and Wonders

There is a belief that God is going to make a great sign for all to see that will convert many. Christians all over the world are waiting for this to happen so that the world will change for the better and also in the belief this may herald the second coming of Christ. Yet when the sun at Fatima seemed to fall from the sky and was witnessed by thousands, the world took little notice. Today, if a great sign were to happen, again it would be explained away and few would take notice.

Christians are not called to wait for signs and wonders *(Mt 12:38-39 'We wish to see a sign from you.' He said to them in reply, 'An evil and unfaithful generation seeks a sign')* but they are called to be that sign, the sign of Christ to the world. God, from the very beginning called mankind into a loving partnership with Him and He is still calling. Christians are meant to go out to the world and by the Grace of God change the world for the better. Christians are not supposed to wait for God to do it but are called to be the instruments God will use to complete His work on earth *(Phil 2:13 For God is the one who, for his good purpose works in you)*. Christians should not be waiting for a sign to change the world but should be striving in the love of the Lord to change it *(Luke 12:43 Blessed is that servant whom his master on arrival finds doing so)*. Seeing the sign of the cross as the only sign they need.

Mini-judgement

As for the mini-judgement when all are supposed to see their souls and hopefully convert, many Christians would be surprised, if this happened, at the state of their own souls. Often people think only of others being judged and forget they will be judged too *(2 Corin 5:10 For we must all appear before the judgement seat of Christ)*.

Mini-judgements are happening all the time throughout the world as souls are touched by the Holy Spirit and converted. People who have had a conversion often talk of seeing how wrong they have lived and how they needed to change. They talk of the desire to love God and to try and live good and holy lives. This frequently happens when a Christian has helped them come to Christ. This is God calling through a servant who has said 'Yes' to taking God's love to others. God has worked through this willing vessel to pour out His grace to convert and heal others. This is the duty all Christians have and many deny, a denial that many will be called to account for on Judgement Day.

The mini-judgement is a continuous process put in place by God, brought about by the Holy Spirit touching souls through those who truly imitate and serve the Son of God, Jesus Christ Our Lord *(Gal 1:12 It came through a revelation of Jesus Christ)*.

Summary

There is so much more that could have been covered in this book but then the simplicity of it may have been lost. There are many more complicated and intricate answers to the questions posed here and I encourage those who want those answers to go and find them through the Holy Word of God, through Church teaching, through what was passed on in tradition and in history.

The answers given in this book may cause some people to question what they have accepted as true, may cause some people to look at society and themselves in a different way but then that is what it is meant to do. The intention is to help bring all people who read this book closer to Our Lord Jesus in their lives and closer to understanding 'What is Truth.'